## Praise for *Creating Wicked Students*

"Paul Hanstedt is a teacher's teacher. He approaches the college classroom with a combination of excitement, experience, skill and humor. His goal—to create 'wicked' students, ready to face the daunting challenges of the twenty-first century—is right on point. And his strategies and recommendations are clear, practical, and instructive. I can't wait to share this highly readable and valuable book with my colleagues."—**Bret Eynon**, *Associate Provost, LaGuardia Community College (CUNY)*

"A must-read for anyone who cares about educating the next generation of change agents. Hanstedt combines practical advice for all college teachers committed to learning outcomes that will help students thrive post-graduation with a thoughtful analysis of what our true jobs as educators should be in a world that is in flux, deeply inequitable, but also in need of many more wicked problem-solvers."—**Debra Humphreys**, *Vice President of Strategic Engagement, Lumina Foundation*

"From its playful title to its final chapter, *Creating Wicked Students* offers a thought-provoking new approach to course design focused on helping college students develop the abilities and self-authorship needed to work—and live—meaningfully. Hanstedt guides the reader through a design process for courses where students learn skills and content, but more significantly, develop 'the capacity to step into a complicated, messy world and interact with that world in thoughtful and productive ways.'"—**Deandra Little**, *Director, Center for the Advancement of Teaching and Learning; Associate Professor of English, Elon University*

"Hanstedt's *Creating Wicked Students* is, as they say in Boston, 'wicked good'—a clear, clever, and creative step-by-step guide to creating courses that help shape students who are ready to engage with and make a positive impact on the world in which we live."—**Michael Reder**, *Director, Joy Shechtman Mankoff Faculty Center for Teaching & Learning, Connecticut College*

"*Creating Wicked Students* places faculty members in the role of engaged learners where the skillful Paul Hanstedt guides them to construct curricula, courses, and assignments that will prepare students to participate in the world in active and constructive ways. Faculty readers become Hanstedt's 'wicked students,' equipped to transfer the skills practiced in this book to challenge their own students to do their best work."—**Amy Sarch**, *Associate Vice President for Academic Affairs, Shenandoah University*

"Hanstedt's conversational tone conjures feelings of sitting with a colleague sharing ideas, brainstorming, and exchanging stories over coffee with lots of laughs. At first, I didn't want to participate in the 'Designing Your Course' sections. But by the first 'Intermission' I was so inspired I was engaging in all activities, ideas pouring out as if attending a great conference. Hanstedt uses his own wicked design within his book, resulting in an overwhelming sense of authority for the reader, indeed demonstrating the power of wickedness."—*Kimberly Whiter, Director of Faculty Development, Jefferson College of Health Sciences*

CREATING WICKED STUDENTS

# CREATING WICKED STUDENTS

## Designing Courses for a Complex World

*Paul Hanstedt*

STERLING, VIRGINIA

Published by Stylus Publishing, LLC.
22883 Quicksilver Drive Sterling, Virginia 20166-2102

Library of Congress Cataloging-in-Publication Data
Names: Hanstedt, Paul, 1965- author.
Title: Designing courses for a complex world / Paul Hanstedt.
Description: First edition. |
Sterling, Virginia : Stylus Publishing, LLC, [2018] |
Includes bibliographical references and index.
Identifiers: LCCN 2017042998 (print) |
LCCN 2017061565 (ebook) |
ISBN 9781620366981 (uPDF) |
ISBN 9781620366998 (mobi, epub) |
ISBN 9781620366967 (cloth : acid free paper) |
ISBN 9781620366974 (pbk. : acid free paper) |
ISBN 9781620366981 (library networkable e-edition) |
ISBN 9781620366998 (consumer e-edition)
Subjects: LCSH: Critical thinking--Study and teaching (Higher) |
Problem solving--Study and teaching (Higher) | Education, Higher--
Curricula. | Curriculum planning. | College teaching.
Classification: LCC LB2395.35 (ebook) |
LCC LB2395.35 .H37 2018 (print) |
DDC 375/.001--dc23
LC record available at https://lccn.loc.gov/2017042998

13-digit ISBN: 978-1-62036-696-7 (cloth)
13-digit ISBN: 978-1-62036-697-4 (paperback)
13-digit ISBN: 978-1-62036-698-1 (library networkable e-edition)
13-digit ISBN: 978-1-62036-699-8 (consumer e-edition)

Printed in the United States of America

All first editions printed on acid-free paper
that meets the American National Standards Institute
Z39-48 Standard.

Bulk Purchases
Quantity discounts are available for use in workshops
and for staff development.
Call 1-800-232-0223

First Edition, 2018

*For Ellen, James, Lucy, and Will*

*Always*

# CONTENTS

# ACKNOWLEDGMENTS

Most scholarship stands on the shoulders of giants. I'd like to begin by expressing gratitude to five of my giants. First, I want to thank Kim Filer, whose wisdom, insight, energy, and ideas were crucial to my ability to move forward with this project. Among other things, she introduced me to the work of Marcia Baxter Magolda, which in turn helped me find a language for topics I have been exploring for the past 20 years.

Next, I need to thank the late Edmond Ko, who first introduced me to the concept of wicked problems and to the idea that students who face wicked problems must have wicked competencies. My sense is that everyone who came in contact with Ko left his company changed. Certainly, that was the case with me.

Thanks also to Gavin Brown, who first introduced me to the idea that as students move into the world, it's possible that they require more than just content and skill, that a strong sense of their right to engage in meaningful discussion may also be a factor.

I must also immediately thank Asia Arnold and Nicole Petty, the two undergraduate research assistants who helped me with this project. It is not an exaggeration to say that this book could not have happened without them.

Additionally, I owe a great deal to my colleagues and the administration of Roanoke College, including but not limited to Chris Bowen, Chris Buchholz, Rachel Collins, Katie Elmore, Justin Garrison, Rich Grant, Wendy Larson Harris, Mike Heller, Katherine Hoffman, Chris Lee, Jonathan Lee, Mike Maina, Sandee McGlaun, Ken McGraw, Lindsey Osterman, Ryan Otto, James Peterson, Robert Schultz, Richard Smith, Gail Steehler, and, I'm sure, a dozen or so others I'm forgetting here but who spark my thinking and push my ideas and challenge me to do better.

I also must thank my brilliant colleagues at the Association of American Colleges & Universities Institute on General Education and Assessment for their support, kindness, and wonderful ideas, Sybril Brown, Helen Chen, Peter Doolittle, Bret Eynon, Ashley Finley, David Hubert, Yves Labissiere, Peggy Maki, Kate McConnell, José Moreno, Terry Rhodes, and Monica Stitt-Bergh.

Thanks also to the Hong Kong gang, including Anita Chan, Joe Chaney, Po Chung, Chris Deneen, Hedley Freake, Gray Kochhar-Lindgren, David Pong, Glenn Shive, William Sin, and Hui Xuan Xu.

Additionally, I'm well aware that much of my thinking over the years has been shaped by passing interactions over dinner or evenings at the pool, so thanks to Amy Balfour, Pat Bradley, Laura Brody, Chris Gavaler, Ellen Mayock, Stacey Vargas, Lesley Wheeler, and Julie Woodzicka.

Finally, many thanks to the folks at Stylus, especially John von Knorring (who must have attended a dozen of my talks and workshops) and the amazing and wonderful and funny and kind and smart David Brightman, who suffered patiently with me as I developed this project, and who always knows where the good restaurants are. Seriously, though, David, you made this possible. Thank you.

# I

# RETHINKING THE WHOLE STUDENT IN WICKED WAYS

This book begins with the assumption that what we all want for our students is for them to be capable of changing the world. The changes they make may be big, or they may be small. They may be political or spiritual or procedural or pedagogical. They may involve a chemical formula or a reading of Shakespeare, the evolution of Weber's thinking, or a development of evolutionary theory. The point is, in the end, when students leave college, we want them to enter the world not as drones participating mindlessly in activities they've been assigned but as thinking, deliberative beings who add something to society.

## Wholeness

Although my thinking on this topic is the culmination of a career's worth of research, teaching, and learning, the ideas in this book really came into focus a few years ago when I heard a college president speak of the features that she said made up the whole student. Expanding on an Ignatian tradition that argues that we need to educate the mind, body, and spirit, this president included three additional elements: emotions, creativity, and . . . well, I have to admit I don't remember what the sixth element was.

Although I understood where this scholar was coming from, my sense was that any construction of students as a culmination of parts vastly misses the mark. Let me put it another way: I do agree that when educating our students we must treat them as more than just names in a grade book. We must recognize that they are complex beings made up of interacting minds, bodies, spirits, emotions, and so on. On some level, we need to design universities that recognize, value, and account for these complexities.

I also believe we can design universities and university curricula that address all these characteristics—and whatever the heck that sixth component was—and nevertheless still send our students out into the world lacking a sense of wholeness, a sense of themselves as fully capable human beings who can have a meaningful impact—sometimes large, sometimes small, but always meaningful—on their surroundings. In fact, I think we do this all the time: Every year, colleges implement agendas intended to make sure students have contact time with curricular and extracurricular features designed to check off the various whole person boxes. And every year, we graduate students who enter the workforce desperate to get a job, desperate to earn a good paycheck, certain that all they need to do to be happy in life is be a good employee and play by the rules, and in short, go out into the world with a stunted sense of their capabilities and of what it means to live a rich and fulfilling life.

Of course, I recognize that academia produces plenty of graduates who have a strong sense of purpose and of their ability, even their right to pursue that purpose. Nonetheless, a lot of our graduates leave campuses with a degree and little else. Indeed, as Arum and Roksa (2011) so eloquently reveal, as far as most students are concerned, the certifying power of the degree is the sole purpose of going to college, besides, of course, the social life. Once they have that degree, they believe they can become part of the workforce, prosper, and be happy. In this context, then, educating the whole student means little more than creating a student who can slide easily into the workforce, participating in the status quo.

## An Alternative Metaphor

In this book I'd like to offer an alternative metaphor for understanding what it means to be whole as well as an exploration of the consequences of that understanding for course and assignment design and pedagogical practice. This approach begins with an incident that took place a few years ago when I was attending a workshop. A department chair stood up and said, "Well obviously, we don't want our students to be the line *workers*, we want them to be the line *managers*."

Although many in the room nodded at this comment, some of us found ourselves pausing, wondering if this was indeed the case. Didn't we, in fact, want our students to be the ones who walk into the room, look at the line managers and line workers, and ask, "I wonder if there's a better way?" or walk into the political debate, look at the entrenched right and the entrenched left and ask, "I wonder if there's a better way?" or walk into a nongovernmental organization and look at the employees and the clients and ask, "I wonder if there's a better way?"

What's more, in addition to asking if there's a better way, I feel that someone who is whole would have an idea of how to go about exploring the current dynamics of the situation, whatever they are, and possible alternative approaches to the situation. And beyond that, this person would have an idea of his or her ability to engage in this process, a sense that the world and the workplace are fluid and ever changing, and all of us as citizens are allowed to participate in these changes in thoughtful ways.

In other words, if we've educated our students effectively, they move into the world as questioning, informed, thoughtful agents of positive change. This isn't to say that they engage in change for change's sake; doing so would erase the word *thoughtful* from the equation. The point here is that wholeness is not quantitative in nature—if you've been educated using X + Y + Z, you are now complete—but qualitative: You're whole, you're complete, you've reached a key level of your essential potential when you understand that you have the ability not just to watch the world but to participate in it, to shape it, to change it.

Thus, when we educate a literary scholar, we expect the scholar to understand the basic skills and methods of that field and to use them appropriately; but finally what we hope is for that scholar to come back to us not simply parroting established readings of texts but adding something meaningful to the conversation, revealing an insight that hadn't previously been noticed. And when we educate a chemist, we expect that person to understand and be able to apply the methods and knowledge of that field; but in the end, our greatest hope is for that chemist to improve the field of chemistry or the work of chemists by discovering, say, a means of developing biodegradable plastic or an environmentally friendly form of motor oil.

Similarly, when we educate a social worker or accountant or psychologist, although we recognize our responsibility to graduate someone who is proficient in the basic tasks of those fields, we are not adverse to the idea that somehow that social worker might find a better protocol for dealing with clients, that the accountant would have the wherewithal to go to a superior if he or she noticed systematic failures in corporate applications, that the counseling psychologist would be capable of transcending known practices to help a client whose symptoms don't necessarily conform to those in the *Diagnostic and Statistical Manual of Mental Disorders*.

It is worth noting the way the issues described here reflect the changing nature of life today. The late Edmond Ko, a key thinker in the field of general education, liked to talk about how his engineering students often faced *wicked problems*, that is, situations where the parameters of the problem and the means available for solving them were changing constantly. "If they're going to face wicked problems," Ko used to say, "we need to give them wicked competencies" (E. Ko, personal communication, May 4, 2010).

Of course, this applies not just to engineering students and engineers but to all students and all workers in all walks of life. 10 years ago, few people anticipated the opening of Myanmar to the rest of the world, the rise of the Islamic State, face-to-face chat on cell phones, legalization of gay marriage across the United States, fake news, or the Zika virus. The parameters are changing. The tools and technologies are changing. We live in a wicked world, an unpredictable world. We need wicked graduates with wicked competencies.

This is an ambitious goal, one that some might see as problematic. After all, is it really our job as academics to engineer social, political, and economic change? And what if a student's goal is simply to get ahead, get a good salary, and fit into corporate (or nonprofit, governmental, or academic) culture?

With regard to the question about engineering change: Perhaps this is not our job. But neither is it our job to create mindless individuals who simply do as they are told. Our world faces complicated problems with the natural environment, the political climate, education, poverty, and technology. We need educated citizens who have a sense of the world around them and of their ability to interact in that world in meaningful ways.

With regard to the question of a student's choosing to assimilate into the status quo, this is also fair enough to ask. But the key here is choice; choices can only be made when people are fully aware they have other options. If a graduate truly chooses to participate in existing structures, that's perfectly fine, but he or she must make this decision with eyes wide open, cognizant that placing self-interest above public need is only one of several available options.

In summary, when we in the academy state that we desire our students to be whole, I believe we mean that we want them to leave college capable of achieving their full human potential to shape and reshape the world—and themselves. Indeed, I would go further and say this is our sole hope for our students: We want them to enter the world knowing they have the ability to participate in thoughtful and constructive ways. To hope for anything less would be, I believe, to acknowledge an essential meaninglessness in our work.

## Authority

All this is a very nice vision, of course; very few would argue with the idea that students should leave college with the capacity to engage in positive change. But how do we achieve it? Almost reflexively, most institutions and academic programs respond to this question with the following simple equation:

$$\text{CONTENT KNOWLEDGE} + \text{SKILL KNOWLEDGE}$$
$$= \text{THOUGHTFUL CHANGE}$$

Although the acquisition of content knowledge and skills is crucial in arriving at the goal of thoughtful change, the kinds of complex challenges we're discussing here require more than that. Simply put, if content and skills were enough, education would already have achieved this goal, particularly after the rise in standardized testing that the United States has experienced over the past two decades.

In the end, content and skill knowledge must be augmented by an attitude, a disposition, a sense of one's ability to enter the world not as a mere cog in the machine but as a thoughtful, competent individual who, when the situation calls for it, is able to step forward to ask questions and propose solutions that may lead to a reinvention of the machine. We might illustrate this idea along the following lines:

CONTENT KNOWLEDGE + SKILL KNOWLEDGE +
ATTITUDE = THOUGHTFUL CHANGE

To a generation of faculty wary of a culture of entitled students, this may seem like a risky venture. It's important to note that the attitude we are after here is more than confidence or agency. After all, one can be confident without necessarily being correct or even informed. Similarly, agency, the ability to act on the world and reshape it, does not necessarily require wisdom or forethought. A 16-year-old driving a car the wrong way down a 1-way street has agency. But certainly we hope for more than that in our students.

Instead, I would like to suggest the term *authority*. Using this word has its problems, so let me get a few things out of the way immediately: When I use the word authority, I do not mean anything related to authoritarianism, arrogance, bullying, bossing others about, or dominating people. Authority in this context is not a word about being at the top of the food chain, being in charge or feeling superior.

Rather, I'm using the word in a way that looks both forward and backward. Authority in this context implies authorship, the ability to write and rewrite, shape, and create. At the same time, this ability comes from something or someone. Authority is granted, given, earned. The content and skills students acquire during their years in college are crucial; they are part of what creates a sense of authority in students. What we teach them matters. As my friend Eric Amsel has put it, in this context authority means mastery of these content and skills. Perhaps, then, we're not looking for a single equation but two simultaneous, even contradictory, equations such as the following:

CONTENT KNOWLEDGE + SKILL KNOWLEDGE
= SENSE OF AUTHORITY

and

## CONTENT KNOWLEDGE + SKILL KNOWLEDGE + SENSE OF AUTHORITY = THOUGHTFUL CHANGE

How we teach our students is also crucial in the development of authority. If what we're talking about is a kind of authorship of the world, it follows that the learning process that prepares students for this kind of active, thoughtful response to the problems we face must allow them to practice these skills. In other words, the only way to truly develop authority is to practice it, consistently, from the start, in ways at first small, then increasingly large. We need to develop authority in ways that are perhaps less complex (although never simple), then increasingly more complex, that allow students to fail, fall down, and pick themselves back up again. Authority should allow students to learn how problems are solved with deliberation, creativity, resilience, and collaboration that allow them to understand that they are capable of solving problems and that solving these problems leads to a rewarding relationship with the world and with themselves.

In short, we need to develop authority in ways that allow students to understand that engaging in this way in a messy world is what it means to live to their fullest capacity as a human being.

## The Nuts and Bolts

So how do we construct curricula and courses and assignments that provide our students not just with the content and skill knowledge they need to perform in our fields but also with the authority that gives them the ability to respond to a complex world?

My experience is that some students arrive at college with this sense already firmly entrenched in their psyche. Some arrive fresh from the military, where they're often forced to accept responsibilities whether they want them or not. Others come from families that seem to throw them into the deep end, essentially telling them, "Here's a problem, you handle it." Still others have involved themselves in cocurricular activities that have pushed their levels of maturity, such as 4-H, or working in inner-city organizations that pair them with older members of the community.

It is worth noting that in all these cases, authority is earned through experience, practice, trial and error, and continued effort that eventually leads to some level of success. It seems safe to say that the best way to create an environment conducive to developing authority in our students is to place them in situations where they *must assume it*. This is a crucial concept for this book and has major implications for designing our courses, so let me state it again: The best way to gain a sense of authority is to practice it in meaningful, content-rich contexts.

In some ways, this is perhaps nothing new. Kuh's (2008) work on high-impact practices revealed that the more students are engaged in particular pedagogies, the more likely they will perform well on the Association of American Colleges & Universities' essential learning outcomes such as assuming personal and social responsibility, integrating knowledge, and so on. Further, his data seem to indicate that frequent encounters with these practices are particularly beneficial to traditionally at risk populations, resulting in greater retention and higher grade point averages.

A glance at the following list of high-impact practices reveals a variety of pedagogical contexts that require the assumption of authority:

- first-year seminars and experiences
- common intellectual experiences
- learning communities
- writing-intensive courses
- collaborative assignments and projects
- undergraduate research
- diversity and global learning
- service- and community-based learning
- internships
- capstone courses and projects (Kuh, 2008)

Undergraduate research by its very name demonstrates increased authority on the part of students. Traditional models held that research is best reserved for graduate students, that students must first acquire a robust and extensive foundation of knowledge before they're ready to step into an applied setting. The emerging thinking in undergraduate research, however, argues that students benefit from acquiring and applying knowledge simultaneously. The result is undergraduates who are active rather than passive in their learning, who get their hands dirty, assume the role of the scientist (or the statistician or the theorist) almost from the start, develop hypotheses, test them, pore over the results, and test again. In short, these undergraduates take on authority from the very beginning.

A well-designed capstone course also asks students to assume a sense of authority, albeit in a slightly different way, pushing them to pull together all their previous learning to address a particular question or solve a particular problem. In such a context, the instructor cannot possibly be the expert; he or she hasn't taken all the classes the students have taken, nor worked on all the projects they've been involved in over the years. The students must assume that authority themselves.

On the opposite end of the educational experience, first-year seminars have a similar effect. Although the term *seminar* is often applied to courses with a small number of students, in the best iterations seminars place the responsibility for course content on the students. Thus, although there might be some lecturing from the professor, a major component of the course should require students to present their own research. In a literature seminar, one student will research and become an expert on Balzac, another on Dickens, and another on George Eliot or on one particular work or aspect of a writer.

The idea that students are not just assuming authority but are assuming it immediately and at levels appropriate for their learning is key to these examples. This first point is crucial. Research shows that using or applying information after encountering it leads to deeper and longer lasting learning. According to Zull (2002),

> Data enters learners through concrete experience where it is organized and rearranged through reflection. When learners convert this data [*sic*] into ideas, plans, and actions . . . things are now under their control, and they are free of the tyranny of information. (p. 40)

At this point, Zull (2002) said, "data" become "knowledge," information becomes meaningful (p. 40). In the context of a seminar, then, students are being asked not to just learn information, or just take it in, but apply it in some way and use it in some way, both of which strengthen their learning and ask them to assume authority. This is in contrast to more traditional constructions of the college classroom. More than once instructors have said to me something like the following: "All this 'active learning' is just fine, but in my class I need a good 10 weeks to get my students up to speed before they can actually do anything." I understand where this is coming from: Certainly, it doesn't make any sense to have students apply no information; that's just bad teaching. At the same time, a traditional model that tells us to lay an extensive foundation before asking students to apply that information (in Organic Chemistry 1, they learn the basics; in Organic Chemistry 2, they apply those basics) assumes a learning process that doesn't actually work for most people. In the end, what we're seeking is a level of "balance" between content and application (Zull, 2002, p. 34).

I expand on this more in the next chapter, but for the time being let me make my first point that when I say it is best for students to begin to assume authority almost immediately in their university education, this is a goal that is not in conflict with good learning. When we ask students to practice authority—to take responsibility for course content, to be something of an expert rather than a passive recipient of the content—we are asking them to engage in practices that will deepen their learning, making it longer lasting and easier to recall.

My second point—that students must adopt authority at a level appropriate to their learning—perhaps needs little explanation. Asking students to adopt authority by performing tasks that are too simple or too difficult for them will be equally unproductive. In the first case, students will not only feel condescended to but they won't gain much confidence from completing simple tasks, understanding that it means little to perform well at a level below their abilities. In the latter case, students facing a task so far above their knowledge level that the chances for success are minimal will likely gain neither knowledge nor increased skills—and certainly not a stronger sense of their own capabilities (Ambrose, Bridges, DiPietro, Lovett, & Norman, 2010).

My experience is that that it's better to ask more of students than less, to push them further than they've ever gone rather than ask them to retread safe ground. After all, the end goal here is to develop students who can encounter unscripted or wicked problems, situations that almost by definition they don't see coming. Turning a page on the syllabus, then, and seeing a problem that at first seems overwhelming and even a little bit frightening is perhaps not such bad training for life after graduation.

## The Purpose of This Book

Kuh's (2008) work with high-impact practices is important in that it demonstrates the veracity of our thinking. Many, if not all, the practices that have been shown to increase the abilities of our students contain elements that increase authority, enriching students' capability to engage in meaningful dialogue with the larger sociopolitical contexts beyond college.

This book is designed to bring this idea down to the level of our everyday, run-of-the-mill courses. If our goal is to develop students' capacity to be engaged and deliberate citizens, what do we need to do in our classrooms? How should we design our assignments and exams? What texts should we assign, if any?

The structure of the book is simple enough: Chapter 2 takes a broad view, asking what goals should drive our work; chapter 3 examines the implications for shaping the classroom and the rhythm of the semester. Chapters 4 and 5 look at assignment or project and exam design. Chapter 6 explores more than 20 day-to-day activities that can enhance authoritative learning. Finally, chapter 7 offers some suggestions on how to assess authority-driven courses in thoughtful, productive ways that will allow faculty to focus on what they care about while also keeping the assessment gods happy.

Scattered throughout chapters 2 to 6 are several steps titled "Designing Your Course" to allow you to apply the information and ideas in each chapter to your own course. Additionally, there are two Intermissions (one after chapter 3, the other after chapter 6). I've included these to create an opportunity for you to put some of the pieces together, because in the end, that's the whole point: Goals can lead to structure, which can lead to assignment design, which can lead to daily strategies. Because there's a lot to keep track of as we go through this process, I've found that it makes sense to have multiple opportunities for the instructor to step back, line things up, see how they work or don't, and consider and reconsider initial ideas. In the end, this sort of application mirrors the deep learning process of the brain and the sorts of discursive revision, reconsideration, and rethinking we require of our students. I strongly encourage you to take a stab at the "Designing Your Course" steps and the Intermissions.

Indeed, although I'm generally resistant to algorithmic approaches to anything and particularly to teaching (a spirit of irreverence that I hope is present throughout the book) I would encourage anyone hoping to design a new course or redesign an old course to go through the book chapter by chapter. Although this kind of deliberativeness can feel wearying at times, I find that it leads to a fulfilling final product, namely, cohesive courses that allow us to focus on what we really care about, shake us up a little bit in terms of teaching strategies, and create assessment data that reflect our values, falling, as Tewksbury says, "naturally out of the course" (B. Tewksbury, personal communication, May 19–22, 2008). Finally, I find that because this process can actually free us from old and sometimes overused approaches, it often results in courses that are a joy to teach.

If, however, you find yourself inclined to skip around, or if you're just looking for a quick fix for day-to-day exercises or assignment design, feel free to ignore the chapter on assessment. I always do. If your course isn't test heavy, you might pass on chapter 5 as well, although I think you'll get a certain level of pleasure in including wicked questions on a final exam. Paradoxically, it's entirely possible to ignore the issue of authority altogether if you so choose and simply use the book as a guide to basic course design, beginning with goals and moving all the way through to day-to-day teaching strategies.

In the end, whatever else you do, be sure to read chapter 2. Although the whole issue of course goals and learning outcomes can be a little ponderous, I find that properly handled in a reasonable way, clearly stated goals for a particular course can really free our thinking, making everything else in designing and teaching the class that much easier.

# 2

# SETTING GOALS FOR OUR COURSES

Because, ultimately, the course you design should be driven by your understanding of your own field, please begin by taking a few moments to work through the following exercise.

---

### Designing Your Course: Step 1

1. Choose a course you'd like to work on. It does not matter whether this course is part of your major, part of the general education curriculum, or offered as an elective. Write down the title of this course.
2. Take a moment and jot a few responses to the following questions:
   - Why does this course matter to the work done in your field?
   - In what ways can the information in your course be used in other fields or other courses?
   - What is unique about the way your field views the world? (B. Tewksbury, personal communication, May 19–22, 2008)
   - What is it you like most about the course and course material?
   - In an ideal world, what would students be able to do with the knowledge and skills they attain in your course? (Diamond, 2008; Tewksbury, personal communication, 2008)

---

I will admit the first time I encountered the concept of course goals, I didn't like it. I'm a humanist after all. I bring students into contact with great works of literature and art, big and important ideas that have changed the world, and various ways of looking at life that can bring meaning to our existence. I like to think I change students' lives. How can I possibly create a goal that captures that, especially when I'm being told I have to prove students are achieving my goals? I need to be able to provide visible evidence of this?

And I've heard other complaints. Colleagues tell me they don't have time for goals, that they've got a lot of ground to cover, saying, for example, "My main goal for this class is to make sure that they're ready for the next class! They need to know this stuff!"

Then there's the fact that at a lot of institutions, a goals-based approach to teaching and learning is dictated from on high, coming to us from an administrator, or worse, an accreditation agency. Goals in this instance are associated with the whole assessment culture, which for many of us feels like a big waste of time. So why bother with coming up with goals for our courses? Why put all this time and energy into something that seems contrary to our own purposes? Over the years I've come to see there's a surprisingly long list of legitimate reasons for doing so. To save time, however, allow me to focus on just two.

First, students are not like us. Years ago a colleague of mine was in a workshop in which the leaders laid out the four types of learners, drawing quadrants on the floor and describing the traits of each corner. Then they asked all the faculty in the room to go to the corner where they felt most comfortable. Telling me this story, my colleague's eyes grew wide as he said, "And then we all went to the same corner! All of us!"

As college professors, we are not normal. We're comfortable with abstractions, we delight in the life of the mind, and we're so motivated by intriguing questions that we do double the graduate work of doctors and lawyers and then take jobs that pay half as much (or less). When we're listening to a lecture or discussion, we're thinking about how the ideas being conveyed connect to concepts we've encountered before, where they might take us in the future, and how we might resolve contradictions between what we're hearing and what we'd previously thought.

But what about most of our students? They're thinking, "Will this be on the test?" and although this sounds condescending, it's not really. After all, most of our students—most, not all—have been taught year after year, in class after class that the test or the paper or the final project and the grade that comes with it are the only things that really matter. And they've learned their lessons well, so well, in fact, that they made it into college. Why change now?

What a goals-based approach to course design does, then, is foreground—to the students as well as to us—the idea that education is about more than memorizing content. Yes, content is crucial but as a means to an end rather than as the end itself. We learn stuff—chemical elements, verbs, equations, policies, concepts—for a purpose, so that we can *do* something with them. And that's where goals come in: What do we want students to be able to *do* with the content we teach them?

This leads directly to the second reason I've come to value a goals-related approach to course design, which is that goals remind us that learning is about more than the reception of information. The past two decades have provided scientists and instructors with a great deal of information about how the brain works on a biological level. Zull (2002) simplifies that research by describing a cycle of learning wherein students first encounter course content as a "concrete experience" (p. 17) through a lecture, a discussion, a reading, a lab, and so on. However, for that information to become deep learning—that is, learning that can be recalled beyond the test—more must happen. Ideally, students will have time to reflect on what they've experienced, will be able to draw up an abstract hypothesis or two, and will be able to test those hypotheses. Zull's diagram is shown in Figure 2.1.

Zull (2002) makes the point that this journey toward deeper, more long-lasting learning is continuous. Active testing, after all, leads to concrete experiences, which begins the whole cycle again. Further, this cycle is not necessarily linear, for although all four components are necessary to deepen learning, some steps will be repeated more than once and might occur out of order (e.g., as a student is hypothesizing, he or she may encounter additional concrete information that changes his or her thinking).

Key to our discussion is what Zull (2002) calls the "transformation line" (p. 40), that moment we already touched on in chapter 1 where data become knowledge (p. 8). Zull places this line between reflective observation and abstract hypothesis (see Figure 2.2). Above this line is input and reflection: We have an experience, encountering new information or ways of thinking

**Figure 2.1.** The learning cycle.

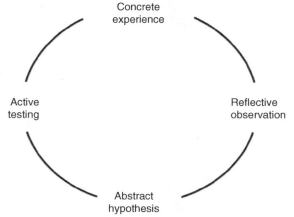

*Note.* From *The Art of Changing the Brain*, p. 17, by J. Zull, 2002, Sterling, VA: Stylus. Copyright 2002 by Stylus Publishing. Reprinted with permission.

**Figure 2.2.** The transformation line.

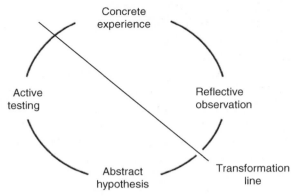

*Note.* From *The Art of Changing the Brain,* p. 40, by J. Zull, 2002, Sterling, VA: Stylus. Copyright 2002 by Stylus Publishing. Reprinted with permission.

we hadn't encountered before. Below this line is action: Based on our thinking about this experience, we *do* something with that information; we test it, connect it, apply it. For many students, however, the process stops short of the transformation line. They'll receive content, for example, taking notes on readings, on lectures, and on discussions. But more likely than not, they won't think about that content very much, connecting it to prior learning, their own lives, or their long-term goals—until, that is, exams take place, at which point the main application that occurs will be wondering whether or not this information will be on the test.

Here again, I would argue that well-designed goals can reshape the learning experience so that it goes beyond mere data collection toward application, testing, and association, and finally, deeper more long-lasting learning.

Stated simply, I believe a goals-oriented approach to designing courses helps ensure that we meet our students where they are and then take them where we'd like them to be. This again plays into the concept of authority: We're not interested in maintaining the status quo wherein students see the university as a certification process to be suffered through before moving on to a paycheck. We're not interested in graduating students who are passive and simply take the world as it is; rather, we're interested in developing students' capacity to be active agents of thoughtful, positive change. A goals-based approach to designing our courses helps us get them there.

Different theorists and practitioners lay out different criteria for what makes a good goal (see Diamond, 2008, chapter 13; Fink, 2013, chapter 2; Wiggins & McTighe, 2005, chapter 3). For our purposes here, I argue that a good goal:

- requires students to actively engage with course content in an authoritative manner, and
- provides measurable evidence that they've done so.

Let's look at each of these separately.

## Designing Authoritative Goals

No one, I assume, will be at all surprised by this. As I've already stated, it's my experience that authority cannot be developed unless authority is practiced. Any goal that allows a student to remain a relatively passive recipient of course content will not do. Consider the following: Three students are assigned a chapter in a book. The first one reads the chapter carefully then makes an outline of the chapter using key words and phrases in the text. The second student finishes the chapter then answers a number of questions at the end, referring to the text when necessary. The third student finishes the chapter then generates a list of questions that might be useful to discuss with the class the next day.

Which student will leave the class with the strongest grasp of the material, or the best chance of being able to recall the material in meaningful moments two days, two weeks, or two months later? Furthermore, which student will leave the course not only with an understanding of the material but with a sense of authority that will allow him or her to actually use that material in meaningful ways—that is, ways filled with meaning?

The answer to both questions is the third student. With regard to the question concerning deeper, more lasting learning, the first student is essentially copying the material: It goes in his or her eyes and out through his or her pen. The brain is not engaged, doing very little other than making sure words are spelled correctly. Any sifting, organizing, or analysis of ideas has already been done by the textbook author. The student is just along for the ride. Most people could do this while listening to loud music or watching television.

The second student is doing only slightly better in relation to deep learning. Chances are when the student answers a question after reading the chapter, he or she will come up with whatever information best presents itself from shallow memory. When that fails, the student will flip through the pages, find the desired material, then copy it down, sometimes word for word, sometimes in the student's own words, condensing ideas and shortening phrases to be able to move on and watch a favorite cooking show or send a text to family members. In this situation, that last part, placing ideas in one's own words, is at least somewhat valuable because it requires sifting, sorting, and evaluating what does and doesn't matter in the text. This is somewhat akin to the reflective observation stage in Figure 2.2. To complete this task, the student will have to think back to the instructor's lecture, a wrong answer on the previous exam, or any other bits and pieces of prior information that might indicate what matters and what doesn't in this particular academic context. At the risk of simplifying a complex neural process, what's happening here is that the student is linking new information to already existing neural networks. Doing so potentially makes it easier to access this new information. Unlinked, new facts are like a train station to which only a single track leads: The information can be retrieved, but only through a limited means. Connected to prior information, however, these new facts are like stations on a complex rail network, with multiple paths leading to the content; there are any number of routes by which the information can be retrieved, and, consequently, that retrieval becomes easier.

The third student takes this process a step further. Deciding what questions to write requires thinking about the material and making decisions about what matters and what doesn't. To do this, students need to recall previous discussions, the types of questions the instructor has asked, previous experiences they've had in other classes where they've been asked questions they found valuable, the ways students in their classes (past and present) have responded to various kinds of questions, the kinds of ideas that have stymied them and their classmates in the past—and on and on and on. Further, in developing the questions the student will be forced to think not only about the past but the future by picturing the class and thinking about peers' responses and about particular answers they might give. Are those answers what the student is after? If not, the student will then revise the questions, again projecting into possible futures. Closer? Yes. Good. On to the next question.

What's happening while the student is involved in this complex process is that he or she is engaging more and more prior knowledge about the instructor, the course and its content, classmates, and his or her own learning. Firing these established networks increases the chances that he or she will be able to recall this information later on. For example, a study by Kole and Healy (2007) demonstrated that students presented with information about famous people they were familiar with were twice as likely to recall that information than students presented with similar information relating to people they didn't know. Further, requiring this student to create questions for the class to discuss increases the chances that the student will not only be mentally engaged with the content but also emotionally invested. Most students (although, sadly, perhaps not all) will want their questions to be good ones that succeed in making their classmates think and will not want to appear inadequate in front of their peers. Chances are, this engagement will also deepen the learning (see, for instance, Zull, 2002, chapter 5).

But let's also consider these three students in terms of authority. The first student assumes very little responsibility for the course material, simply following what others have done. The second student assumes some authority by attempting to answer the questions and taking responsibility, recognizing that he or she is the one who has to do the work. But deep down, what's driving this student is knowing there are correct answers to these questions and that the student's job is simply to *find* these answers, not create or develop answers or take risks and try to argue for a distinctive answer that is perhaps counterintuitive—simply find the "right" answer.

In contrast, the third student is, well, choose your metaphor. Driving without a map? Swinging on a trapeze without a safety net? Stepping off the edge? Yes, this student is applying prior knowledge of the professor, the text, classmates, and other classes, but that knowledge is only partial. The student must move into new territory alone, and, moreover, he or she knows it.

The beauty of requiring students to adopt an approach like this is that it mirrors and prepares them for the complexity of real problems in the real world. What we have here is a wicked problem, perhaps not the wickedest problem in the world, but wicked nonetheless. And to solve it, the student needs to adopt and refine and develop, over time, wicked competencies and move beyond the (partially) known into new territory.

But I'm getting ahead of myself. More of these types of day-to-day pedagogical strategies are covered in chapter 4. For the moment, the key idea is that the type of learning in which the third student is engaged is more likely to happen if we're deliberate about creating goals that push students to assume authority.

But how do we do this? The key is to select productive verbs for our goals that enable students to practice wicked competencies. A helpful tool in this process is a taxonomy developed by educational psychologist Benjamin Bloom (1956) and his colleagues in the 1940s and 1950s. *Bloom's Taxonomy*, as it has come to be known, essentially breaks down the thinking and learning process, starting with the most basic of the cognitive functions—acquisition of knowledge—all the way up to more complex practices. Later, Krathwohl (2002) revised Bloom's work, retitling some of the categories and reordering two of the higher level processes, placing *create* at the very top. As with Zull's (2002) cycle of deep learning, in many ways this chart and these verbs are simply metaphors for an infinitely complex process of learning. Nevertheless, this system is useful in that it can help us understand what we're asking of our students, and more important, push our students toward wicked competencies. The entire taxonomy is shown in Table 2.1.

**TABLE 2.1**
**Krathwohl's Taxonomy (Krathwohl, 2002)**

| Remember | Comprehend | Apply | Analyze | Evaluate | Create |
|---|---|---|---|---|---|
| Define | Classify | Apply | Analyze | Appraise | Arrange |
| Describe | Defend | Change | Break down | Argue | Assemble |
| Identify | Describe | Compute | Calculate | Assess | Categorize |
| Label | Discuss | Dramatize | Compare/Contrast | Choose | Combine |
| List | Distinguish | Employ | Criticize | Compare/Contrast | Compose |
| Memorize | Explain | Illustrate | Diagram | Conclude | Construct |
| Name | Identify | Interpret | Differentiate | Defend | Create |
| Outline | Locate | Manipulate | Discriminate | Discriminate | Design |
| Recognize | Paraphrase | Operate | Examine | Estimate | Develop |
| Relate | Predict | Predict | Experiment | Evaluate | Devise |
| Recall | Recognize | Prepare | Infer | Judge | Formulate |
| Reproduce | Review | Produce | Model | Justify | Generate |
| Select | Select | Relate | Question | Interpret | Plan |
| | Summarize | Schedule | Relate | Predict | Prepare |
| | Translate | Show | Select | Rate | Rearrange |
| | | Sketch | Separate | Select | Reconstruct |
| | | Solve | Subdivide | Summarize | Reorganize |
| | | Use | Test | Support | Revise |
| | | | | Value | Rewrite |
| | | | | | Set Up |
| | | | | | Synthesize |

A few points warrant discussion here. First and foremost, some of the terms in the taxonomy appear in multiple categories, such as *identify*. As is perhaps self-evident, this occurs because words have multiple meanings, and the same action can occur on different levels. Thus, a student could be asked to identify the main characters in a novel, which is a simple task of remembering names, or be asked to identify the major motivations for these characters, a much more complex action. A more extreme example is the verb *summarize*, which occurs at the Comprehension or Understanding level and later at the Evaluation level. It's easy to understand why this occurs. Asking a student to summarize the plot of a short story is much easier than asking a student to summarize the key points of the president's State of the Union address as it relates to matters of foreign policy in Asia. The first requires some fairly basic skills, whereas the latter requires the student to sift through a great deal of information, prioritizing and cutting and collecting, based on a particular set of complex criteria.

In the end, it's crucial for instructors to be honest with themselves. We know when we're using *compare* in a relatively simple way and when this term demands more careful, perhaps even riskier thought. If our goal is to engage students in complex and authoritative thoughts and actions, we need to begin by holding ourselves to high standards.

This leads to a second, very important point: Two things distinguish the verbs in the first few columns on the left-hand side of Table 2.1 from the verbs in the columns on the right. First, the verbs on the left generally don't engage students in cognitively complex ways. Second, the verbs on the left generally allow students to remain relatively passive; authority is pretty much eschewed. The farther you move to the right, on the other hand, the more cognitively engaging the described action becomes and the more learning is deepened, becoming longer lasting and easier to retrieve. Simultaneously, generally speaking, the farther you move to the right, the more you are asking students to engage in the kinds of thinking that prepare them for the challenges of a wicked world.

Consider, for instance, the following goal from a nutrition course:

> By the end of the course, students will be able to identify the key components of a comprehensive wellness plan.

Although this goal might make sense for the early weeks or even days of a course, it hardly encapsulates the sorts of hopes for our students that drive our work or the kinds of challenges they'll face once they graduate. Yes, these basic concepts are important, but we don't spend 14 or 16 weeks a year prepping every night so that students can perform tasks that a reasonably well-trained eighth grader with access to the Internet might be able to do.

The following goal presents a nice contrast:

> By the end of the course, students will be able to construct a personal nutritional plan appropriate for their age, body type, and lifestyle.

This goal pushes students toward the right side of Krathwohl's (2002) taxonomy: Creating something that didn't exist before from a variety of components, some of which come from the class, some that may require some research, is a cognitively challenging task. It will take more time and more practice. Furthermore, this goal is closer to replicating a wicked problem: Students will have to juggle lots of complex material and apply it in an equally complex context. Clearly, here they're moving off the edge of known content and into a more fluid realm. Even if they can find material directly relating to their age and body type, *lifestyle* complicates the task, bringing into play everything from ethnicity and region to religion and social habits. Thus, it will require careful analysis, evaluation, and synthesis of a great deal of information.

It is important to note the way this second goal illustrates Tewksbury's (Personal communication, 2008) argument that higher-order goals (that is, the more authoritative goals on the right-hand side of Table 2.1) often have embedded lower order skills. In other words, a student cannot synthesize course materials unless he or she has mastered them. I discuss this more momentarily, but suffice it to say that this is important because it reminds us that high-order goals are not a replacement for the basics but rather a means of taking foundational material to a more productive level of learning.

The following is another high-order goal from a general education course examining the relationship between science and religion:

> By the end of the course, students will be able to compare and contrast the philosophies of science and religion.

This is a nice example because it shows how something that could be quite low order (comparison and contrast) can actually be a very complex task when applied to dense intellectual material. Contrasting religion and science on a superficial basis would be easy. But comparing, looking at what they have in common, will push students beyond many of the things they're encountering in the media, in church, and in their homes; they'll have to step back and look carefully at the underlying concepts that drive these very different (or not so different?) modes of thought.

An additional goal from the same course takes this even further:

By the end of the course, students will be able to analyze how the philosophies of science and religion shape our lives.

Here again we see the attributes of an effective high-order goal. The basics are implied (you must understand these differing philosophies to apply them), but the brain is engaged in a complex task that will require more than mere or rote copying. Furthermore, as with the previous nutrition example, the learning here is not just an end in itself but a means of understanding the world.

This idea of connecting to life beyond the classroom is crucial for a number of reasons. For one thing, goals like this deliberately integrate course content into prior knowledge, to preexisting neural networks in the brain. As a result, recalling this new information becomes easier. Second, a goal like this makes it easier for students to understand the relevance of course content to life beyond the classroom. As Arum and Roksa (2011) so eloquently point out, one of the real challenges of tertiary education today is that students often view it merely as a means of certification, a way of upping their pay scale. As such, education for them becomes a formality, a hoop to jump through, as opposed to a means of gaining knowledge and ways of thinking that will enrich and advance their lives and work. What goals of this sort do, then, is knock down the wall between college and the world beyond the classroom, pushing students to explore how the two connect.

But does this goal enable authority? Maybe not. But that's okay. Although I adamantly believe there are steps we can take to structure our syllabi and classroom practices to better enable students to step into the world as more active participants, I don't necessarily think everything we do has to serve that goal. We have other agendas. I've seen too many people take an approach to course design that's algorithmic, almost dictatorial, as if there were one way to do things and only one way. The fact is, our work differs from field to field, our institutions are different, and we serve different student populations. Furthermore, we come into this work because we care deeply about our fields and our students; we have a passion for these things. Given the minimal number of extrinsic rewards in our work, we need to respect our intrinsic motivations and pay them due diligence. As Robert Diamond (2008) puts it, we need to be careful to avoid anything that reduces "instructional excitement" (p. 157).

Nonetheless, I strongly believe that goals will be more effective—both for the students and for us as we design our courses—when drawn from the right-hand side of Krathwohl's (2002) taxonomy in Table 2.1. The farther you move to the right of that table, the more engaged and challenged your students will be, the more they will learn and remember, and the more they will be able to act on what they've learned, either in future classes or once they've graduated.

Not surprisingly, some faculty find this idea discomforting. "What about," they'll say, "the basic skills? I don't know about *your* field, but in *my* field there's foundational information that students absolutely need to know before they can go on to more complicated tasks." Fair enough. Here's what I suggest: First and foremost, remember that high-order goals often have implied lower-order tasks. Thus, a student can't effectively analyze a work of literature (high order) without a grasp of the basic terminology of the field (low order), the sociohistorical context of the work (low order), and the ways words can have meaning on multiple levels in multiple ways (medium to high order, depending). In other words, if I create a goal that says, "By the end of the course, students will be able to analyze an unfamiliar piece of literature to reveal multiple cogent meanings," I've already committed myself to teaching the lower-order skills or, more accurately, to making sure my students learn those skills. Thus, actually creating goals that address these lower-order skills seems unnecessary and even a little redundant.

Beyond that, note that one of the tangential benefits of writing course goals is that they provide us, the instructors, with a useful shorthand. Before the semester starts, it's easy to put together a syllabus that makes perfect sense to us. In the middle of the semester, with exams and papers to grade, classes to prepare, and committees placing demands on our time, sometimes this perfect sense disappears. "What was I thinking?" we'll ask ourselves as we glance at the 12th week and wonder how on earth we're going to cover X without first having covered M, which doesn't show up in the reading until 3 weeks later.

One tactic I'd suggest involves explicitly "nesting" content in high-order goals. For example, say the following is a high-order goal for a literature course:

> By the end of the course, students will be able to analyze an unfamiliar piece of literature to reveal multiple cogent meanings.

This goal might then be followed by the following list of skills, ideas, and content that the student needs to master to achieve high-order thinking:

- master literary terminology
- understand historical and social contexts

- be able to analyze words for connotation, denotation, and multiple meanings

The following example is taken from a physics course exploring kinesiology. Note that here, when listing the nested features, the instructor has simply listed the concepts:

By the end of the course, students will be able to predict the effects of the following on various human movements

- force
- pressure
- position
- velocity
- friction
- gravity
- density

In each case, the instructor has begun by creating a high-order goal that fully coincides with his or her best hopes for the students. The initial goal is intellectually demanding, pushing students into grayish territory where they're going to have to work beyond simple memorization or even simple application. Then the instructor created a bullet-point list of the various lower-order skills and concepts necessary for achieving that goal. This is a useful approach for instructors because it reminds us that content is not the end of the course, only the means; it allows us to use high-order practices in our classroom, pushing our students toward deeper forms of leaning; and it can clarify in the midst of a busy semester how the various parts of the course fit together.

Some instructors even like to put these nested items on their syllabi. Often, they'll do this in a parenthetical form that takes up less space, for instance: "By the end of the course, students will be able to predict the effects of various human movements (force, pressure, position, velocity, friction, gravity, density)." These faculty find that this approach is effective in foregrounding for students the connectedness of the course content—the idea, in other words, that the knowledge students are acquiring on a day-to-day and week-to-week basis consists not of isolated concepts but parts of a whole. Students who understand they're learning for a real purpose rather than for a test will be more highly motivated. Further, as Ambrose and colleagues (2010) point out, structuring goals like this might help students better understand how to organize information, which in turn can aid recall (more on this in chapter 3).

---

### Designing Your Course: Step 2

Take a moment to consider the following questions, being sure to jot down a few notes:

1. Looking at the verbs on the right-hand side of Table 2.1 (under Apply, Analyze, Evaluate, and Create), which ones stand out for you?
2. Look at these same sections of this table and note which verbs seem best suited for the work people do in your field.
3. What are some of the high-order thinking skills or tasks you would like to see students perform in your classroom? What verbs might best work with each of these tasks?
4. Finally, what lower order skills or basic contents are necessary for performing these tasks? Briefly list them, then place each of them below the various high-order goals you developed in number 3. Don't be afraid of repeating the same contents or skills with multiple tasks. That's perfectly normal, and that repetition leads to greater learning.

---

## Creating Measurable Goals

In many ways, creating goals that are measurable is one of the more challenging parts of the course design process. The reasons for this are often complex, but I have found they boil down to these two issues:

- the development in the past decade of an administrative culture of assessment that is often frustrating and even demeaning for faculty and
- an idealism that often shapes the way we faculty think about learning.

Regarding the first of these, suffice it to say that as public pressure to justify rising costs in tertiary education increases, the demands administrations have placed on faculty have increased twofold. "Give us numbers!" faceless voices shout from administration buildings across the country. "Any numbers! Just give us proof that your students are learning so we can get (choose your demon here: accrediting agencies, state governments, parents) off our backs!" It doesn't help that very often when we hand over the requested data, these voices seem to disappear into a vacuum, and we don't hear a peep from the administration until the next year's numbers are due. In such a context, it's not surprising for faculty to become cynical about a call for verifiable goals that will lead to clear proof of learning.

In the face of these arguments, the only point I wish to make—and keep in mind, I've happily not been an administrator for 20 plus years now—is that barring some miracle, the pressures that gave rise to assessment zealotry are not likely to go away. In the face of that, our goal as instructors is to ensure as much as possible that the assessment process and the goals we create reflect a boots-on-the-ground understanding of our field and the needs of our students. Put another way, done right we should be able to create measurable goals that match our own purposes for teaching and our greatest hopes for our students. Keeping the assessment monsters happy by giving them the numbers they want? That's just a bonus.

The second issue, our idealism and the way it shapes our concept of learning, is more complicated. Rather than address this matter immediately, I'd like to set it aside for a moment to create a clear understanding of what I mean by *verifiable* or *measurable* goals. Consider the following goal:

> Students will be able to think critically about mass media's representations of science.

On the face of it, this is a perfectly reasonable goal; indeed, some would say it essentially captures our greatest hope for higher education, which is creating a population of graduates who don't simply accept the world as presented to them by the media in all its forms but who question these representations and consider not just what is but what could be.

The problem here is that the achievement of this goal is difficult to verify. We can't just ask students, "Are you thinking critically?" All of them, one eye on the grade book, will of course say yes. What we need is a means of gathering evidence that our students can do what we ask them to do. We need to have something we can see or hear that lets us know that yes they are thinking critically or no they're not. Thus, perhaps a better way of stating this goal might be:

> Students will be able to analyze a contemporary scientific debate as portrayed in the media, distinguishing between evidence and conclusions and evaluating the validity of the latter.

Granted, this is a much wordier version, but at least it clarifies critical thinking for this particular context: being able to sort through unwieldy quantities of media content, make distinctions between data and conclusions, and evaluate the latter for validity.

Furthermore, this goal lends itself to verification. Students can produce something, a paper, an oral presentation, or the answer to an exam question, that shows they can do what we're asking them to do. As instructors, being able to gather evidence like this is invaluable. As Christopher Deneen points out, what is being verified here is student learning and pedagogical practice (Deneen & Hanstedt, 2011): If we end up with a course in which 86% of our students can meet our goals, then the degree of learning validates our approach to teaching, the texts we chose, the labs we require, and so on. If, on the other hand, only 30% of students can do what we've asked, it's likely we need to reexamine our approach, because there is something going on that extends beyond the odd 1 or 3 students with attendance problems (Deneen & Hanstedt, 2011). Making changes to our courses can take time; before committing to them we want more than just a vague impression that things are not working. We want evidence.

Here's another goal:

> Students will be able to understand the importance of the Impressionist movement.

Again, we have a perfectly reasonable goal, at least in terms of its content. Impressionism brought to the forefront of society a shift in artistic methods that had a lasting influence on the art that followed. What art history professor (or general education humanities professor, for that matter) wouldn't want students to comprehend this?

Unfortunately, there are several problems related to this goal. First and foremost, it's vague: What do we mean by *understand*? Does it mean students can repeat the main points of a lecture or reading? That they can analyze in detail the influences Monet's cathedral paintings had on, say, the poetry of Ezra Pound? These are two very different things. The first is low order, basically requiring memorization and the ability to paraphrase; the second requires the ability to pull apart the Impressionist technique, abstract it, transfer it to a literary context, and then apply it to the dense works of an often opaque writer.

Chances are most professors will argue that the latter explanation of *understand* is what they're after. Students will be able to analyze complex ideas and apply them in new settings. But if that's the case, perhaps it would be better to simply create the following goal:

> Students will be able to analyze Impressionistic goals and methodologies as they evidence themselves in contemporary art and literature.

This goal is much clearer, stating explicitly what the faculty member really wants from the students. Additionally, as with the previous example of critical thinking versus distinguishing and evaluating, this version better enables verification, providing the instructor with a method of gaining evidence that students have or have not achieved the goal.

Additionally (and looking forward to chapter 4), these goals provide something of a road map toward assignment design. The phrase "understand the importance of the Impressionist movement" give us no hint about where and how a goal will be tested. "Impressionistic goals and methodologies as they evidence themselves in contemporary art and literature," in contrast, reminds us of exactly the sort of question we will need to ask on an exam or in an essay prompt. And because we know at the very start of the course the sort of question we'll be asking in week 10, we now have the ability to shape how the course is structured as a whole (e.g., include a few small contemporary works on the syllabus?) as well as some of the day-to-day strategies of the course (maybe conclude a discussion of the causes of Impressionism by asking if any of these pressures still remain in today's world?). I discuss these matters in more detail in chapters 3 and 6, but suffice it to say that creating goals that are verifiable is valuable not only for the assessment hounds in college administration but also for ourselves, helping us think more deliberately about the overall shape of the course.

## Using Our Idealism to Create Better Courses

This leaves only the matter of idealism to discuss. Very often when I'm leading a workshop on course design and I get to the matter of verifiable goals, someone will raise a hand and say, "Maybe that works in the sciences, but what I'm teaching in the humanities can't be measured" or "Maybe that works in the humanities, but what I'm teaching in the sciences can't be measured" or "Maybe that works in the humanities and the sciences, but what I'm teaching in the social sciences can't . . ." well, you get the point.

Although it's tempting to dismiss this as a polite form of resistance, I'm more inclined to see this issue as stemming from our deepest hopes for our students. After all, few of us got into this profession to become number crunchers, and even the statisticians and accountants among us have higher hopes for our students than that they become adept hoop jumpers. We're not just creating data, after all; we're shaping complex human beings who will leave our classrooms after four years and move into the world, reshaping themselves and their culture and society in ways that are difficult to anticipate.

Given all of this, it's not surprising that we're occasionally tempted to write goals like the following:

Students will adopt part of Native American philosophy to their lives.
Students will learn to think like physicists.
Students will find a poem that changes their lives.
Students will appreciate the complexity of social interactions.

Although some might smirk at one or another of these—Find a poem? Really?—I always feel just a little bit better when I encounter draft goals along these lines. For implicit in phrases like these are, I believe, our best intentions for our teaching, our greatest hopes for our students—in a word, our ideals.

Unfortunately, for our purposes here, goals like this create a myriad of problems. Most obviously, they're difficult to measure. How can we judge if a student truly appreciates anything? How will we know if a student has found a poem or painting or formula or philosophy or theorem that will change a life that has only begun? How exactly do scientists think, and how do we know when they're thinking and when they're not?

Not surprisingly, when you tell people their ideals don't make very good goals, they tend to get a little irritated. And needless to say, removing this drive from the course design process is detrimental. Indeed, doing so would likely and rightly lead to complaints that the administration, the assessment people, or the course design coordinator is reducing the potential of the course, forcing the instructor to create rinky-dink syllabi consisting of shallow benchmarks and meaningless checked boxes.

In response, I simply point to the previous section of this chapter in which I'm encouraging all of us to create high-order goals that will push our students to greater, more expansive actions that demonstrate a mastery not just of course content but of the competencies required in today's complex world.

But I recognize as well a tension between the kinds of high-order thinking we're after in our best moments of teaching and the sort of verifiable concreteness we're talking about here. Figure 2.3, developed with Christopher Deneen, a colleague in Singapore, demonstrates one method of negotiating this tension.

Assume for our purposes that the circle in Figure 2.3 represents our highest hopes for student learning in our courses. Contained in this circle are our wishes that students become inextricably fascinated with the content of our courses and leave our classrooms and lecture halls determined to become chemists or poets or political radicals. Whatever drives us to teach in a career with long hours and relatively mediocre pay is in that circle.

**Figure 2.3.** Our ideals.

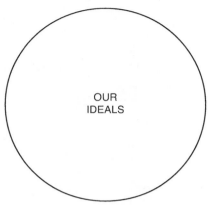

Now assume that Figure 2.4 represents the contrast between our ideals and what is measureable. The outer circle continues to represent our greatest ambitions for student learning in our class. The inner shaded circle represents what is actually measurable. Obviously, there's a gap. Our ideals expand well beyond what we're actually able to measure. We can't provide evidence that our students have become inextricably fascinated with our courses, that they are determined to become chemists, or that they'll engage in widespread political activism. Nor, for that matter, can we prove they've found a poem that will change their lives, that they're now thinking exactly as a scientist would, or that they've adopted Native American philosophy in their lives.

**Figure 2.4.** Our ideals versus the verifiable.

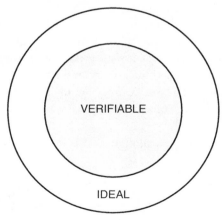

**Figure 2.5.** Pushing the limits of the verifiable.

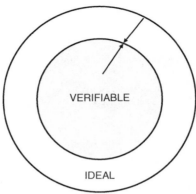

It's important to note, however, that the two circles in Figure 2.4 obviously overlap a great deal. There is much within our idealistic realm that can be verified. Indeed, I would argue that our best hopes for successful course design come with a willingness to exploit the tension between the inner and the outer circles. More exactly, I believe that the key to writing an effective goal is to push the limits of what is verifiable, aiming for that liminal zone where what is ideal and what is verifiable meet (see Figure 2.5).

Consider, for instance, the colleague who hopes that students would adopt part of Native American philosophy to their lives. This is a perfectly reasonable desire for an instructor to have, albeit one that is difficult to measure. Further, it's not unlikely that the sort of adoption this instructor is hoping for would come later in life, once students have settled into the complexities of the adult world and have come to see the value of some of those abstract ideas they were forced to read about way back in college. Indeed, my guess is that most of us have received e-mails from students who graduated a decade earlier, thanking us for insisting they learn something that in the intervening years has become increasingly important to them. But of course the only way we know that our course had an impact is if a student bothers to write, hardly the sort of sample size we want to rely on when making decisions about curricula.

Consider the possibilities, though, if this instructor wrote the following goal:

> By the end of the course, students will be able to articulate the value of Native American philosophies for contemporary life.

With a goal like this, the instructor could then create an assignment (or an exam question) that asked students to do the following:

Construct a plan spanning at least the next 10 years in which you incorporate Native American thinking into your everyday life. Be sure to cite and carefully analyze the complexities of at least three of the texts we've worked with this semester.

What would happen with a goal, and a subsequent assignment, like this? First, the instructor would get a full sense of the extent to which his students understood these philosophies. As with the nested outcomes mentioned earlier in this chapter, basic understanding, a low-order goal, is essential for the student to perform the required task.

Second, students would be pushed to apply these abstract concepts to the world around them. In doing so, students would be increasing the number of neuronal networks their brains are firing. Rather than using an isolated set of networks connected only to the course, students would be linking course content to preexisting networks related to the world outside the classroom, to their personal and professional goals, to how they hope to approach life after graduation. This connection to prior knowledge and prior ways of thinking is, as I've mentioned before, essential to deep, lasting learning.

Third, I would argue that a goal (and an assignment) of this sort increases students' sense of authority: An assignment like this makes clear the idea that we have agency in shaping our own lives. We can adopt philosophies, reject ideas, and turn away from what those around us expect of us. In many ways, this matches Marcia Baxter Magolda's (1999, 2001) concept of self-authorship, the idea that students should be able to define their own belief systems. For many students, this is a surprising and very powerful notion. Too often they see themselves as the product of their circumstances. Although of course we can't ignore the strong socioeconomic factors in play in all our lives, surely we hope for more from our educational systems than the idea of students as products, shaped but never shaping, acted on but never acting deliberately and thoughtfully.

Related to this, I would argue that by creating a goal of this kind and a subsequent assignment of this sort we've increased the chances that the instructor's most idealistic goal—that students adopt elements of indigenous philosophies in their own lives—has become increasingly likely. Using a traditional course design model, where the instructor simply delivers content and students make of it what they will, the chances that students would finally adopt elements of Native American thinking in their own lives is essentially random: Students with a predisposition toward this kind of thinking may well adopt. Other students might get lucky, coming into contact with the right idea at the precise moment when it's meaningful to them. The rest? Well, they will do what they always do in their courses: Memorize the material for the test, take the test, hand in the test, and move on.

Requiring all students to complete an assignment of this kind, however, creating what Diamond (2008) refers to as an "observable" (p. 153) action, makes certain that all students take the abstract concepts in the course and applies them to their own lives. As a result, more students will see how these concepts might enhance their lives. Some might adopt them immediately; others, perhaps not at all. Still others might suddenly find themselves 6, 10, 15 years down the road in a situation where these same practices they'd written about all those years ago are suddenly applicable. And because they'd written about them and thought about how those practices might be useful, their recall and their ability to apply those practices in the current situation would be increased.

All of this is really more the topic of chapter 4, which focuses on assignment design. The larger point here is that we don't have to sacrifice our ideals when we take a goals-based approach to course design. Almost every goal we have for our students, and I would include the big goals that cause us to take up the mantle of our fields, can somehow be refined and pushed toward that liminal zone so that it becomes verifiable. The result of this push, I would also argue, is a better goal that deepens learning and increases the chances that our students actually end up with the kind of long-term thinking and skills we want them to have.

In support of this idea, I offer the following revisions of the other idealistic goals previously mentioned.

Students will learn to think like a physicist

becomes

Students will be able to distinguish between evidence and conclusions and evaluate the validity of the latter.

Meanwhile, the literary goal:

Students will find a poem that changes their lives

becomes

Using close analysis, students will be able to argue for the value of poetry in the contemporary world.

A unique feature of this literary goal is the opening clause, "Using close analysis," wherein the instructor lays out what Diamond (2008) refers to as "the conditions under which the action takes place" (p. 153)—that is, how the student will go about proving he or she can fulfill this goal. A phrase like this is useful in that, like nested goals, it creates a sense of coherence between the skills and content of the course and the long-term aims of the course. As such, the value of the skills and content are foregrounded, a key factor in motivating students (see Ambrose et al., 2010, chapter 3).

One final example: Still drawing from the original list of ideals, consider what might happen if we reworked the goal,

Students will appreciate the complexity of social interactions

into

Students will be able to apply the basic concepts of sociology to analyze actual social interactions in a complex way.

In many ways this is just a matter of rewording, replacing the verb *appreciate*, which is hard to observe and measure in a reliable way, with *apply* and *analyze*, which are actions that students can either do or not do but that we most definitely can observe. Also noteworthy is the way the phrase *basic concepts* is used, embedded as it is in a high-order setting. Once again, students will see that memorization of foundational terms and concepts is just a stepping-stone toward more important work, the kinds of applications and thinking that make taking a course like this important for life in the real world.

And again, although authoritative efforts aren't necessarily a part of any of these revised goals, these goals nonetheless prepare students for assuming an authoritative stance. After all, we're not interested in having students solve complex problems related to social interactions if they can't first effectively analyze the situation using the best thinking from the social sciences or the natural sciences or the humanities.

One effective trick faculty might employ to further prepare students for the wicked workplace and beyond comes from Barbara Tewksbury. In her excellent course design tutorial, she places a premium on asking students to work in settings and with data that are new to them (B. Tewksbury, personal communication, May 19–22, 2008). The previously revised goal could easily be reconstructed as the following:

Students will be able to apply the basic concepts of sociology to analyze *unfamiliar* social interactions in a complex way.

An outcome of this sort really pushes students to use all the modes of thought that are essential to the social sciences, particularly the ability to observe carefully in an objective way. Indeed, one could argue that emphasizing the new and unfamiliar is perhaps the single best means we have of preparing students for life after graduation, particularly in a world where the problems we'll face haven't yet been anticipated, and the tools we'll use to solve them don't yet exist.

Finally, I want to revise the initial thesis to this chapter and argue that there are not two but *three* keys to creating effective goals for our courses. We need to design goals that accomplish the following:

- require students to actively engage with course content in an authoritative manner,
- provide measurable evidence that they've done so, and
- engage students on a level that enacts our greatest hopes for them.

## Aligning Our Goals With Institutional Goals

I'll be frank. At this point I'd like to stop and move on to exploring how the goals we create can help us better shape course structure and assignment design. For many of you, that would be just fine. Because of the way you

---

### Designing Your Course: Step 3

1. Go back to your notes from Steps 1 and 2; what stands out to you?
2. What can students create, analyze, exhibit, or perform that will capture the spirit of your highest aspirations for them?
3. Using this information, draft three to five goals for your course. Feel free to embed basic contents and skills in each goal. As you draft your goals, remember the three keys to effective goals, which should do the following:
   - require students to actively engage with course content in an authoritative manner,
   - provide measurable evidence that they've done so, and
   - engage with students on a level that enacts our greatest hopes for them.

---

work or the way your institutions conduct assessment, you don't really have to worry about issues of alignment. If that's indeed the case for you, feel free to skip this final section.

For the rest of you, I'll make this as quick and painless as possible. Further, let me assure you that contrary to common wisdom, you can indeed have your cake and eat it too.

Here's how: I think another reason instructors dislike outcomes-based course design so much is that we're often handed prefabricated goals from our institutional or departmental mission and told, "This is what you will

teach in your courses." Besides rubbing against our innate desire for autonomy, this can grate on us because the goals we're handed are very often of the
lowest common denominator, generic and bland and about as inspiring as
a pot of two-day-old soup, along the lines of "Students will become careful
readers of literature" and "Students will be able to apply appropriate methods
to solve problems."

My point here is not that these are bad goals. Deep down, they have
their merits. But these institutional and departmental goals often seem to
prohibit the kinds of creative, thoughtful, robust, invigorating goals we've
been discussing thus far in this chapter. And this can be frustrating, because
we're also told that finally we will be held accountable for fulfilling the institutional goals.

Before I respond to this challenge, it might help to make sure everyone
has a clear sense of what administrators and the institutional assessment people are thinking about when they're asking for data (see Figure 2.6).

Different institutions, regions, and countries use different terminology,
but essentially Figure 2.6 illustrates the logic—in a very simplified form—
administrators and accrediting agencies are using when they assess whether
a university is doing what it says it's doing. Every school has a mission statement that gives rise to more particular goals for student learning. Department
administrators then choose which outcomes they are prepared to address.
Courses taught in those departments are assigned (or instructors choose) particular goals that are appropriate for the topic and content. Some institutions
have additional steps: Some universities comprise schools—professional, arts
and sciences, commerce, and so on—and many departments have multiple
majors or programs. For example, a business department may offer degrees in
marketing, economics, accounting, and management. These additional features require additional layers in the assessment and accreditation processes.

**Figure 2.6.** Basic institutional alignment.

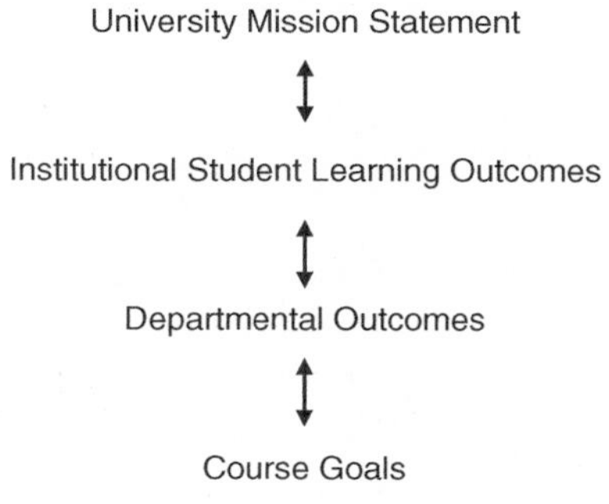

University Mission Statement

$\updownarrow$

Institutional Student Learning Outcomes

$\updownarrow$

Departmental Outcomes

$\updownarrow$

Course Goals

**Figure 2.7.** How institutional goals become course goals.

Institutional outcomes
Students will be able to read, listen, and observe carefully

Departmental outcomes
Students will be able to apply the skills of critical reading to texts of literary and cultural
significance.

Course goals
Using close analysis, students will be able to argue for the value of poetry in the
contemporary world.

Nonetheless, the overall logic is the same: The institution as a whole must be able to demonstrate that its mission and campuswide student outcomes are being met at the course level. Which brings us back to the point of this section of this chapter. Inevitably, despite our best intentions and all our hard work, we may feel pressure from the institution to align our carefully crafted and idealistic goals with its (often) poorly crafted (by committees) and (mostly) generic goals.

My first response to this situation is to point out that as often as not, it's easy enough to nestle our personally designed course goals into the generic institutional goals. Take for instance, the flow chart in Figure 2.7, developed using materials from my own institution. I've skipped the mission statement so that I could focus on the departmental level.

As the student learning outcomes move from institution to department to course, they become decreasingly generic and increasingly specific to the course and the instructor. Thus the institution's directive to read carefully becomes a department's analysis of literature (as opposed to, say, a sociology article), which then becomes a course goal requiring the use of close analysis to argue about the value of poetry in the contemporary world.

Note that the individual course does not have to fulfill every aspect of the institutional goal, that is, reading, listening, and observing. Note as well that the individual course can, and, I'd argue, should have additional specifics that contextualize and give greater meaning and clarification to the goal. In other words, course goals can go beyond the minimum standard set by outcomes higher up in the food chain. No rule says we have to settle for the lowest common denominator. As long as we meet that minimum goal—careful reading—we're giving the institution what it wants and needs.

My second response is similar, although on a slightly larger scale. Simply put, there is no rule that says instructors can't have goals that have nothing to do with institutional and departmental outcomes. Here again, as long as we meet the minimum goals that we must achieve to keep the administrators

---

### Designing Your Course: Step 4

1. Take a moment to look at your departmental goals.
2. Which of the goals you've created for your own course naturally align with your departmental goals?
3. Are there departmental goals that are not being met by your course goals? If so, quickly draft a few course-based goals, doing your best to meet the following standards we've repeated throughout this chapter:
   - require students to actively engage with course content in an authoritative manner,
   - provide measurable evidence that they've done so, and
   - work with students on a level that fulfills our greatest hopes for them.

---

happy, we're good. Any goal we have beyond that should not be a problem. So, although my department may require me to ensure that students can read, write, and think critically, I may also have a goal that states that students will be able to work productively in the digital humanities or that students might be able to engage in visual rhetoric. As long as I'm giving the department or institution what it needs to keep the assessment agencies happy and I'm teaching to attain all my course goals, things should be fine.

## Sample Goals

The following goals were developed from my own work and a variety of other sources. Some are perfect, some are not; some are authoritative, some are not. However, all of them illustrate what is possible and may spark your thinking.

Social Sciences

- Students will be able to develop and test age-appropriate lesson plans (B. Tewksbury, personal communication, May 19–22, 2008).

- Students will be able to assess the ramifications, positive and negative, of industry and technology on individuals and society using course readings, discussions, and research as a foundation.

- Students will be able to analyze a contemporary problem from multiple perspectives, constructing a solution and rationale that takes into account the complexity of the issue.

- Students will be able to evaluate educational research critically and participate in the research community (Tiu & Osters, 2005).

- Students will be able to apply structured and semistructured interviewing techniques in their fieldwork ("Student Learning Outcomes," 2015).

- Students will be able to develop an individual learning plan for a child with learning disabilities ("Student Learning Outcomes," 2015).

- Students will be able to produce a strategic plan for a small manufacturing business ("Student Learning Outcomes," 2015).

- Students will be able to locate and critically evaluate information on current political issues using the Internet ("Student Learning Outcomes," 2015).

- Students will be able to apply sociopsychological principles to suggest solutions to contemporary social problems ("Student Learning Outcomes," 2015).

- Students will be able to work in a group to achieve agreed-on goals ("Student Learning Outcomes," 2015).

Natural Sciences and Mathematics

- Students will be able to frame a hypothesis and formulate a research plan (B. Tewksbury, personal communication, May 19–22, 2008).

- Students will be able to analyze an unfamiliar epidemic (B. Tewksbury, personal communication, May 19–22, 2008).

- Students will be able analyze the cultural, agricultural, and socioeconomic factors of a particular region then develop a balanced diet accordingly.

- Students will be able to adapt and apply efficient sorting and searching algorithms to large complex data sets.

- Students will be able to use theoretical techniques to analyze and choose the correct algorithm for a particular problem.

- Students will be able to analyze complex data sets and develop mining and drilling recommendations.

- Students will be able to apply their knowledge of statistics to analyze reports and claims in the popular press.

- Students will be able to propose one or more hypotheses that plausibly suggest how different species can occupy the same ecological niche and support the hypothesis with convincing evidence (Gardiner, 2008).

- Students will be able to apply principles of evidence-based medicine to determine clinical diagnoses and formulate and implement acceptable treatment modalities (Tiu & Osters, 2005).

- Students will be able to design a website using HTML and JavaScript ("Student Learning Outcomes," 2015).

Arts and Humanities

- Students will be able to analyze the influence of a particular piece of literature on contemporary culture and thinking.

- Students will be able to analyze the complexities of identity construction in Chinese art.

- Students will be able to analyze literary concepts in the context of popular movies or television shows.

- Students will be able to articulate the relevance of Socrates and Confucius to citizenship in a globalized society.

- Students will be able to apply knowledge of postcolonial theories to analyze and evaluate the concept of identity in a globalized age.

- Students will be able to construct incisive questions about a literary work and answer them in a thesis-driven essay.

- Students will be able to develop a personal action plan in response to the complexities of humankind's relationships with animals.

# 3

# STRUCTURING
# WICKED COURSES

The other day, a physicist friend was working in the lab with her summer research students. They were talking about the work they'd been doing that summer and about how there was no manual or instructions of any sort for any of it: no textbook, no lab procedure. It was as if they were making it up as they went along. Laughing about this, one of the students said, "You know what we need? We need an entire course with nothing but problems. Just give us one problem after another, and we figure out how to do them. Because that's what *real* research is."

The rest of the students laughed. And then all of them nodded.

## Some Key Assumptions About Structuring Courses

I'm tempted to end the chapter right here. Because if we want to create wicked students who can go off on their own and respond thoughtfully to complex problems, the best way to do that is to give them wicked problems over and over and over again and ask them to solve them.

Sure we need to be in the room with them, at least part of the time, even if that room is, on occasion, virtual. We have to be sure they have the resources they need to solve these problems, and we need to be willing to occasionally ask questions that will get them thinking in a different direction, or give them tips when they're just plain stuck and their frustration is overriding their ability to think clearly. (Sometimes, perhaps, the best tip is to take a break and do something else, or go for a long run.) So we need to be there to support them.

For students to assume authority over course content, though, they must work with that content, they must struggle with it and fail with it and make some progress with it and then more progress and then more progress.

Indeed, I would argue for this not just for gaining authority but, as I pointed out in chapter 2, in terms of basic learning. To gain deep learning, students must actually apply course content, they must do something with it.

This leads us to *Key Assumption 1* when it comes to thinking about how we structure courses: If we wish for students to learn content deeply and develop a capacity for wicked thinking, we have to structure our courses in ways that ask them to do the kind of authoritative work we do in our own fields.

We also need to be in the classroom with students so that we might raise the bar. In other words, we have to order the problems we present to students in such a way that each problem builds on the previous one. The best metaphor I've encountered for course design comes from Barbara Tewksbury (personal communication, May 19–22, 2008), who talks about a conical spiral: Students will go past the same point on a compass repeatedly, performing and practicing crucial skills a number of times, gaining the repetition necessary to, in cognitive terms, move those skills out of working memory and into executive function. At the same time, because of the conical nature of this spiral, every time students repass a given point in their learning, they'll be doing so at a higher level. The problem they will face or the text they will read or the social experiment they will analyze will be more complicated than the previous one.

All of this leads to *Key Assumption 2* with regard to structuring our courses: The degree of difficulty of this work increases as the course progresses. This second point perhaps seems obvious: Of course the material should get harder, right? And certainly in some fields it does. The textbooks used for Physics 101, for instance, tend to build on information from chapter to chapter, so that generally it would be difficult to do the work in chapter 4 if you hadn't read and understood chapter 3.

In many fields, however, that's not the case. Think about a typical textbook for Literature 101, Psychology 101, or American History 101. Sure, the book begins with some introductory material that's essential for understanding the subject, and yes, there are moments in these texts when one chapter builds on another in instances of increasing complexity. But generally, the material is nonhierarchical and the second chapter is no more or less complex than the fifth or seventh chapter. This is particularly true in fields where the body of content that must be covered is growing exponentially. Psychology and literature are good examples of this.

One of the consequences of this sort of structure is that students are left viewing course content as a series of discrete facts. From the student's perspective, chapter 5 may not seem to be related in any meaningful way to chapter 8, which is not related in any meaningful way chapter 11. All of which, of course, feeds into students' assumptions that education is simply about memorizing facts to be regurgitated at appropriate moments to get a grade. Students don't necessarily recognize the ways the information they're taking in is meaningful. And as Ambrose and colleagues (2010) point out, when students view course content as discrete parts rather than as information in relationship to other information, it tends to impede recall.

This lead us nicely to *Key Assumption 3:* When structuring courses, we need not necessarily follow the layout of our textbooks. This point may be a bit more controversial, so I will spend a bit more time on it. If you're anything like me, the pull to cover content is very strong. As a scholar of Victorian literature, I want to share with my students as much of my own learning as I possibly can. I want them to leave the course having read as much Victorian literature as I can reasonably cram into the semester. After all, the more content covered, the more they learn, right?

Unfortunately, two things tend to undermine this thinking. First, teaching and learning are two entirely different things. Just because the content has been covered in a course—through lectures, discussions, or reading—doesn't necessarily mean it's been learned by students well enough to last beyond the final exam. In chapter 2 I discussed Zull's (2002) assertion that application of learning is a key component to long-term retention. We should not only hear a lecture or see a reading; we need to then do something with that information that strengthens the neuronal network, connecting new learning to prior learning. With only so many hours in a given course in a given semester, a course structure that focuses on content delivery over application limits the brain's ability to recall that information later on. And if our courses matter—and all of us believe that they do, otherwise why would we do this?—then we need to adjust that balance to ensure that deep learning occurs.

The second argument against content-driven course design is that we simply can't cover everything our students will need to know. The world and technology are changing rapidly. The challenges we're facing and the tools we'll use to solve them are also changing rapidly. By the time a textbook hits a student's desk, it's been in production for at least two years. If the students are in their first year, by the time they graduate, the thinking, ideas, and content in that book will be at least six years behind the times.

So the bad news is that we can't cover everything. The good news is that we recognize that, and by focusing on authority-based course design, we're doing everything we can to prepare our students for this changing world.

I mention this issue of content coverage up front because in course design it tends to be a major bugaboo. As professors, we take pride in our broad and deep knowledge in our fields. We value that knowledge. We love that knowledge, and we want to instill that knowledge in our students. As a result, we tend to think that activities that take up class time and get in the way of content coverage are a waste of time. It's easy for us to think that way because we've already mastered that content. Indeed, most of us learned in a content-heavy environment. If it worked for us, why shouldn't we do the same for our students?

Well, because most of our students are not like us. It's safe to say that most professors are highly autonomous in their learning, interested in high levels of abstraction, and intrinsically motivated when it comes to their fields. This is not the case for most of our students. Some of them simply view our classes as a hoop they have to jump through. Others don't understand what all the fuss is about, why these ideas are so much more important than, say, real life; and others just struggle. They may have come to college without the tools we had or without the preparation to master high levels of thinking and reams of content. Almost all of them have been shaped by a testing culture that puts an emphasis on content mastery over conceptual thinking. And while content mastery is crucial, we need our students to be able to do something with that content. What's more, we want them to be able to do something not just with the content we cover but with the content we can't prepare them for, that hasn't yet been invented, thought of, or discovered.

Years ago I was at a conference when a colleague came up to me and said, "You have to talk to this guy from Austin College! They've got this great first-year seminar that gets them these amazing results! Their National Survey of Student Engagement data is through the roof." So I sat down with this professor—his name is Robert Cape—and I asked him about Austin College's first-year seminar and about the results. Then I asked him again and again and again. Because even though their data on student engagement showed great outcomes in the first year, the course Cape was describing didn't seem particularly innovative. Finally I said, "I'm confused: What you're describing here sounds like an extremely vanilla first-year seminar. I don't understand how you're getting these results."

Cape nodded, then said,

> When I'm helping faculty develop their first-year courses, I have two iron-clad rules: the first is that their seminars be intellectually challenging. They should demand that students ascend to great heights. The second is that once they've put together their syllabi and included everything they want in the course, each instructor should go back and pull out one quarter to one third of the content. That way, they have the time to teach their students how to learn. (R. Cape, personal communication, 2007)

Content matters. But it will only get our students so far, and we need to force ourselves to remember that as we begin to put together our courses.

In the end, the content we include in our courses should be driven by our course goals, not by what we were taught as undergraduates 20 years ago and certainly not by the table of contents of a mass-market, lowest-common-denominator textbook.

Finally, then, *Key Assumption 4*: Pure content coverage will only get our students so far; we need to make space in the syllabus for learning.

## Rearranging the Pieces of the Puzzle

So how do we achieve our ends? If we are to avoid creating syllabi by opening our textbooks and copying the table of contents, what should we do? Let me demonstrate some options by structuring and then restructuring one of my own courses titled Composition Theory and Practice. Its basic purpose is to teach people how to teach writing. Many of the students who take the course are in education; others are preparing for graduate school in English knowing they will likely have to teach first-year writing. Still others take the course because they are interested in issues of language, identity, and power.

Without even trying too hard, I can think of at least the following five ways to structure this course:

1. By *category*: in my course, this would mean examining the various modes or genre of writing, that is, exploring the kinds of papers my students may teach their students how to write
2. Using *chronology*: in the context of composition theory and practice, this would require following the evolution of thought about how to teach writing
3. Through *methodology*: for instance, when teaching this course, I might focus on the process of writing, first reading and discussing brainstorming or idea generation, then drafting, then revising, then polishing, editing, proofreading, and so on
4. *Theoretically*: by exploring the major schools of thought on writing—in my mind, process, expressivism, and social epistemology
5. By examining *use*: in the context of my course, this might mean looking at the various student populations with which my students might work: elementary, secondary, tertiary, or English as a second language

I like some of these better than others, and I recognize that I've left some things out (digital media, for instance). The point is, when I look at the complex array of content in my field, I understand there are multiple ways of organizing that content.

The first of these, *categorical,* refers to arranging content by type, class, family, division, and subdivision. Using this method I see myself creating a course structured like a number of boxes, each more or less self-contained: personal writing first, then comparative writing, and so on. In other fields, though, I recognize that this approach would end up looking more like the roots or branches of a tree, with each major category dividing and then subdividing into more and more smaller limbs—domain, kingdom, phylum, class, order, and so on.

The *chronological* approach simply looks at what comes first within the course content, then second, and so on. I would assume that causality and reaction would be included in this approach: How did what comes first lead to what comes second, if at all? In what ways is the third section a reaction or response to what came before it?

The third approach, organizing by *methodology,* allows us to think about and explore how problems are solved within a field. In a writing course, this means examining the steps one might take when writing a paper, thinking about how we might teach those steps, and then exploring how we might help students move beyond those steps when necessary.

The fourth approach looks at *theories,* the major ideas driving a particular field. How do those trickle down into day-to-day practices? How do those theories overlap or contradict each other? What major questions do they create?

---

### Designing Your Course: Step 5

1. Take a moment to create a list of all of the content you're inclined to bring to your course. Include ideas and theories, facts and information, major works or artifacts, anything that comes to mind. Don't worry if there seems to be too much, as you can always trim later.
2. Think about the various ways the content on your list might be connected. Draw a few preliminary arrows between items on the list, maybe circle and cluster various ideas, or perhaps draw double lines between paradoxical or contradictory information.
3. Now organize this information in at least three different ways. Feel free to use any of the methods I've mentioned: *categorical, chronological, methodological, theoretical,* and *use.* But also feel free to develop a taxonomy that feels natural or relevant to your field.
4. Take a moment to jot down notes next to each structure, What are the pros of each? What are the cons?
5. Set aside these notes for the moment.

The fifth approach is organized around the various *uses* of the course content. For my course on teaching students how to teach, this means thinking about when, where, and why students will use the information they've picked up in the class. Will they be using the content when working with younger students? With older students? What will they need to know working with these various populations? What will they need to improvise? What skills and content can I give them to prepare them for what we can anticipate, and what resources can I point them toward for those moments that no one yet knows are coming?

There are, of course, many other ways of organizing the overall structure of this particular course and, I've no doubt, methods, ideas, and structures relevant to other fields that are well beyond my knowledge and understanding. What finally matters, though, is that these richer, more connective approaches to course content help students better understand the relationships between ideas and details they might otherwise see as discrete, and understanding these relationships makes that information easier to recall and use down the road (Ambrose et al., 2010).

## Using Our Goals to Create Course Structure: The Simple Version

Once we understand that content can be organized and reorganized in a variety of ways, many of which might help our students move beyond the idea of content as educational detritus, we have greater freedom to structure our courses in ways that allow us to transcend a mass-produced textbook and our own educational experiences, developing approaches that are appropriate for the particular population of students at our institutions and that help these students achieve the goals we developed in the previous chapter.

Returning to the five structures I contemplated for my composition theory course, it makes sense that I should choose a structure that relates to my goals. Were my major goal that students be able to *articulate the various schools of composition theory and evaluate them for their strengths and weaknesses*, then the fourth approach, the *theoretical* one, would be appropriate. Similarly, this approach would work for another of my goals, which is for students to be able to *analyze the social, political, and personal implications of writing in the academy and beyond*. Although both of these goals relate to practice—that is, the day-to-day teaching of writing—the emphasis is on the ideas driving our practices and the social, economic, and psychological implications of those ideas and practices. Consequently, structuring a course based on process or *methodology* wouldn't make much sense. What I'd probably do instead is shown in Table 3.1, in very broad terms.

TABLE 3.1

**Composition Theory and Practice: The Theoretical Structure**

| Week | Course Work |
|---|---|
| Week 1 | Introduction to the course |
| Weeks 2–5 | Theoretical approach 1: Writing process as science (or pseudoscience?) |
| Weeks 6–9 | Theoretical approach 2: Expressivism |
| Weeks 10–13 | Theoretical approach 3: Social epistemic theory |
| Week 14 | Wrap-up and final project work |

I like this approach because it emphasizes the importance of theory in the course; so often students come in just wanting teaching tips and techniques. But these tips and techniques have implications in terms of student development and identity. What works for a privileged child at a private school might be detrimental to a child who has just immigrated or to a child from a poor region in Appalachia.

I also like this approach because it allows me to begin with more basic ideas and end with more complex ones. The process approach to teaching writing is relatively easy to grasp. Social epistemology, with its basis in Marxism and rhetorical theory, is more challenging. It makes sense to approach the latter only after students have begun to develop a working knowledge of the field and have settled in and become comfortable with their classmates and my methods of instruction.

On the other hand, if one of my major goals was for students to *analyze their own writing process*, then it would make sense to give my course a *methodological* structure, first exploring and working with the invention stage of writing, then moving on to the drafting stage, and so on. The basic structure of my course would look something like Table 3.2.

Here again, this approach would foreground for students my priorities. In this iteration of the course, process is what really matters. As a result of this approach, process becomes the connective tissue for all the other content in the course. This approach takes the various techniques I would have students explore, the various theories I would insist they learn, as well as their own writing practices, and puts them together in a way that makes sense out of the material.

Simply put, I'm advocating that when structuring your course, take a careful look at your goals. Do they present a meaningful structure for course content, one that reflects your own priorities in the course and helps students make sense of all the information we're throwing at them? If so, then go with that structure.

**TABLE 3.2**
**Composition Theory and Practice: A Methodological Structure**

| Week | Course Work |
| --- | --- |
| Week 1 | Introduction to the course |
| Weeks 2–3 | Coaching invention |
| Weeks 4–6 | Coaching drafting |
| Weeks 7–10 | Coaching revision |
| Week 11–13 | Coaching proofreading and editing |
| Week 14 | Wrap-up and final project work |

## Using Our Goals to Create Course Structure: The Less-Simple-but-Really-Not-That-Complicated Version

Of course, it's also possible that we have multiple goals that lend themselves to multiple structures that may at first appear to work against one another. Indeed, in my composition theory course I have *both* "Articulate the various schools of composition theory and evaluate them for their strengths and weaknesses," *and* "Analyze their own writing process" as course goals. The first begs a *theoretical* approach, whereas the second lends itself nicely to a *methodology* approach. What to do? Simple—prioritize. Which goal is most important to you? Let that goal to determine the structure of your course.

However, this does not mean the other goal will not be attained, or that the content related to that second, lower priority goal need be excluded from the course. What will happen instead is that the second (and possibly third and fourth) goal will simply be subordinate to the major goal.

To demonstrate, let's say I chose as my main priority the schools of critical thought driving the field, in other words, the goal that students are able to *articulate the various schools of composition theory and evaluate them for their strengths and weaknesses.* In that case, one option is to allow that goal to provide the dominant organizing structure for the course, as shown in Table 3.3.

This still allows me to bring into play my second goal: I want students to be capable of analyzing their own writing process. For that, I would structure the course as shown in Table 3.4.

Basically, I'm subordinating *methodology* to *theory*; that is, each time I bring a different theory to the course, I ask students to go through the process again. When exploring expressivism, we might read an article by Donald

Murray on writing conferences and coaching the revision process. For social epistemic theory, I might have students work together to resolve the conflict in the editing stage between providing academically appropriate works and erasing one's own language.

Indeed, I'd point out that this approach allows me to meet other goals as well. Because I'm preparing students to teach writing, one of my goals is for them to develop a number of practical strategies for the classroom. This fits

TABLE 3.3
**Composition Theory and Practice: The Theoretical Structure**

| Week | Course Work |
|---|---|
| Week 1 | Introduction to the course |
| Weeks 2–5 | Writing process as science (or pseudoscience?) |
| Weeks 6–9 | Expressivism |
| Week 10–13 | Social epistemic theory |
| Week 14 | Wrap-up and final project work |

TABLE 3.4
**Composition Theory and Practice: A Theoretical Structure That Includes Methodology**

| Week | Course Work |
|---|---|
| Week 1 | Introduction to the course |
| Weeks 2–5 | Writing process as science (or pseudoscience?)<br>Invention<br>Drafting<br>Revision<br>Proofreading and editing |
| Weeks 6–9 | Expressivism<br>Invention<br>Drafting<br>Revision<br>Proofreading and editing |
| Week 10–13 | Social epistemic theory<br>Invention<br>Drafting<br>Revision<br>Proofreading and editing |
| Week 14 | Wrap-up and final project work |

very nicely with the structure laid out in Table 3.4. As they work through the process relative to each theory, they ask themselves what strategies they might teach their students at each step of the writing process to enact each theory.

The more I look at this structure, though, the more I'm beginning to wonder if it really places emphasis where it's needed. Does it put my students in the position to really learn the most complicated materials in the course? After all, the methodology part isn't really that hard; it's the theory that students often struggle with. So why repeat the process component over and over again when it's relatively easy to grasp? Wouldn't it make sense to instead have students repeatedly explore the theory as it is articulated through the writing process? Indeed, it would! See Table 3.5.

Using this method, the complex material in the course—*theory*—is hit multiple times, giving students more opportunities to struggle, ask questions, understand, and master. Further, the most complex skill in the course, turning theory into practice, is practiced repeatedly, allowing students to take

TABLE 3.5
**Composition Theory and Practice: A Methodological Structure That Includes Theory**

| Week | Course Work |
|---|---|
| Week 1 | Introduction to the course |
| Weeks 2–3 | Coaching invention<br>Process theory and practice<br>Expressivist theory and practice<br>Social epistemic theory and practice |
| Weeks 4–6 | Coaching drafting<br>Process theory and practice<br>Expressivist theory and practice<br>Social epistemic theory and practice |
| Weeks 7–10 | Coaching revision<br>Process theory and practice<br>Expressivist theory and practice<br>Social epistemic theory and practice |
| Weeks 11–13 | Coaching proofreading and editing<br>Process theory and practice<br>Expressivist theory and practice<br>Social epistemic theory and practice |
| Week 14 | Wrap-up and final project work |

missteps, stumble, figure things out a little, figure things out a little more, and finally start to move toward mastery. I also could see increasing the degree of difficulty for my students by insisting on more and more independence as the semester went along. In other words, early in the course I might be offering them a few examples to get their thinking going and spending a lot of time in class getting very hands-on with student work, making suggestions and asking directing questions. As they moved into the later units, however, I might not provide any examples at all, asking them to generate their own, and then critique these ideas and those of their peers, essentially assuming the role of frontline evaluator. In this way, students would be moving toward greater self-reliance and greater authority.

Given my course, its content, my students, and my goals, I think I like this second approach better. But that's not the point. Rather, I'd like you to take from this discussion an understanding of the following four points:

1. We have multiple options when it comes to how we structure our courses.
2. We can choose an option that foregrounds *meaningful* ways of thinking about the course content, that is, ways that make sense of all the various content and skills we're throwing at our students.
3. We can choose an option that fits our goals for our students and that reflects our own priorities.
4. Just because we foreground one goal doesn't mean the other goals get lost.

In the end, you're the one who knows your course material. Trust your priorities when looking for a structure that makes sense for your students and your course content.

Two final notes before I ask you to engage the next step in the course design process: First, keep in mind that not all your goals will be met through structure. This is okay. As we see in the next two chapters, students will achieve a great number of the course goals through their major projects and exams. This is as it should be, reflecting our understanding that learning involves doing. The way we structure our courses will help students, sometimes a great deal, but it's not the end in and of itself.

Second, it's not uncommon when working through a course-design process like this that faculty begin to feel some frustration with the structure of their textbooks: what they, the faculty, would like to do in the second unit of their course is found in bits and pieces in chapters 3, 7, 11, and 14 in their texts. How on earth can they assign reading in such a fragmented way?

I'm sure there are many possible responses to such a dilemma. Here are three: First, assign the fragmented reading by pulling bits from one chapter and bits from another and explain to students why you are doing this, why you have decided to structure the course as you have, what you see as the relationships among the various ideas covered, and why you think your organizational structure is more meaningful than the one the textbook uses. As Ambrose and colleagues (2010) point out, faculty have a rich understanding of the relationships in the content that our novice students do not have. Taking the time to foreground the relationships that we see between and among various bits and pieces of information is one nascent step in moving our students toward expertise (Ambrose et al., 2010).

A second option is to get rid of our 300-page textbooks and replace them with one or more smaller, more focused works that provide us with the flexibility to use our chosen structure. These smaller works might include any number of journal articles, popular books related to our field, or more scholarly works. One added benefit of this approach is that it might allow us to structure the course in a way that effectively moves students from simpler reading to more complex reading.

Furthermore, it's not out of the question that these smaller works have a level of eloquence that is often lacking in mass-produced, mass-marketed textbooks. Indeed, given the bland writing style of many textbooks, it's no surprise that so many of our students skip the reading. Assigning shorter books geared to the general market might improve our students' reading habits and skills, which in turn might improve their writing skills.

A third option is do away with a course textbook altogether. Essentially this is a flipped classroom approach, which requires students to work on course content outside class through online materials (produced by the professor or others) such as videos, online articles, websites, and other digital resources. Most often, this material is chosen and assigned by the instructor; however, one variation is to set up a course blog or wiki and ask students to crowdsource course material. For example, if the class is discussing Max Weber on Tuesday, by midnight on Sunday every student should find and provide the link to one reliable source on Weber. By midnight on Monday, all students should have commented on at least three of their peers' links. On Tuesday, class begins by asking students to prioritize the content they found and commented on as the instructor takes notes on the board: What's most important about Weber? Why? How do we know that? Among other things, this provides an opportunity for us to talk with our students about reliable as opposed to unreliable online sources, a conversation that in this digital age should take place in every class, every semester.

In the end, I consider moving away from mass-produced texts a good sign: It means that we're paying attention to the needs of our students and to the goals we have for those students. It means we're breaking free from traditional educational approaches that may have worked for grad-school bound students like ourselves in a more closed academic context two decades ago, but that may no longer work for today's university population, a population that is more diverse, less prepared, and more distracted by social media and a cultural narrative that equates education with certification. In other words, shoving aside our textbooks may mean that we ourselves are becoming more deliberate about what we're doing in the classroom. And that's nothing but good.

---

### Designing Your Course: Step 6

1. Take a moment and reexamine your goals. Do any of them seem to provide a meaningful structure to the course that would help students achieve an understanding of how the course contents relate to each other?
2. Now take a look at the three organizational models you created earlier in this chapter. Do you see any congruity among your goals, particularly the more high-priority ones, and your organizational models?
3. If so, take that organizational model and develop it a little further, adding various skills and ideas and content that seem appropriate for the different sections of the model. Consider yourself done, at least for the time being, with this step.
4. If you do not have a model that works or that could work with some simple tinkering, then go back to your goals, choose one goal you really value, and make a sketch of what a course might look like foregrounding the priorities of this goal.
5. Do the same for a second goal.
6. Now do the same for a third.
7. Make notes on each model, exploring the strengths and weaknesses of each.
8. Finally, choose one model and develop it a little further, adding various skills and ideas and content that seem appropriate for the different sections of the model.
9. Move on to the rest of this chapter, knowing that: a) you can always change your mind later; and b) there is no such thing as a perfect course organization.

## Only Connect

The last part of this chapter relates to *Key Assumption 1* presented earlier: If we wish students to learn content deeply and develop a capacity for wicked thinking, we need to structure our courses in ways that ask them to do the kinds of authoritative work we do in our own fields.

With that goal in mind, I'd like to provide two different models for what I consider to be integrated courses, that is, courses that connect, continually and in explicit ways, the learning of the course content with the tasks the students will be required to do in the course and with the world beyond the classroom. Neither of these models is particularly shocking—chances are, you've heard about both of them before, quite often. Nonetheless, I chose to include them here because in my mind they are superb examples of how we can simultaneously deepen our students' learning and increase their authority.

### *Case Studies*

For our purposes, I'm defining *case studies* as a series of real-life problems, professional or otherwise, around which a course is structured. As an example, Jessica Olin at Genesee Community College teaches a first-year seminar that examines animated cartoons as a reflection of society. The major goals for the course are to analyze the content and presentation of animated cartoons and then compare the results between the United States and Japan (J. Olin, personal communication, Jan. 8, 2014). The three case studies around which she has designed the course are shown in Table 3.6.

Key to the case study model is the way in which the abstract concepts and methodologies of the field are connected to examples that are not only concrete, but extended. Unlike a textbook, which might use four different

TABLE 3.6
**Course Design Using Case Studies: Cartoons As A Reflection On Society**

| Week | Course Work |
|---|---|
| Weeks 1–5: Case Study 1 | *Looney Tunes*, including "Baseball Bugs," "Fast and Furry-ous," and "What's Opera, Doc?" |
| Weeks 6–10: Case Study 2 | Japanese anime movies, including *Spirited Away, Death Note,* and *Sailor Moon* |
| Weeks 11–14: Case Study 3 | Student-selected animated cartoons, including *Angry Beavers, Cowboy Bebop*, and *Ed, Edd, and Eddy*; students can choose anything |

examples in a single chapter (not unlike what I'm doing here), the case study approach gives students time to settle into a particular data set, be it numeric, narrative based, or historical. Olin chooses to introduce her first goal, analyzing content and presentation of the cartoons, with her first case study. This analysis is performed applying methodologies adapted from rhetorical analysis and cultural studies, tools that are not particularly intuitive, so Olin chooses to first bring them into play with material familiar to most of the students. Once her students have a solid grounding in those skills, Olin moves to her second and third case studies, layering in additional goals. Finally, the course outline resembles Table 3.7.

Using three separate case studies, Olin allows her and her students time to attend to each of the goals. Additionally, because the earlier goals are repeated, students get multiple opportunities to learn and practice skills that are crucial to the course. And finally, because the goals are layered one over the other, this repeated practice becomes more complicated as the course progresses.

I'd like to point out two things here. First, unlike some of the case study designs I show you later, Olin doesn't necessarily require her students to complete a formal assignment at the end of each data set. In this example, the various cartoons are used largely to clarify ideas and concepts that are practiced in an informal, guided manner.

TABLE 3.7
**Course Design Using Case Studies: Cartoons As A Reflection On Society, With Goals**

| Week | Course Work |
|---|---|
| Weeks 1–5: Case Study 1 | *Looney Tunes* <br> Goal 1: Analyze content and presentation using methodologies of rhetorical analysis and cultural studies |
| Weeks 6–10: Case Study 2 | *Japanese anime* <br> Goal 1: Analyze content and presentation using methodologies of rhetorical analysis and cultural studies <br> Goal 2: Compare and contrast U.S. or Western cartoons to Japanese or Eastern cartoons |
| Weeks 11–14: Case Study 3 | *Student-selected animations* <br> Goal 1: Analyze content and presentation using methodologies of rhetorical analysis and cultural studies <br> Goal 2: Compare and contrast U.S. or Western cartoons to Japanese or Eastern cartoons <br> Goal 3: Generate and execute a research question based on critique and observation of a chosen cartoon |

Second, Olin's texts for the course include nontraditional books by K.S. Sandler (1998), *Reading the Rabbit: Explorations in Warner Bros. Animation*, and S.J. Napier (2005), *Anime From* Akira *to* Howl's Moving Castle*: Experiencing Contemporary Japanese Animation*. As I said, nontraditional course design often separates itself from traditional choices in texts.

Another example of a case study design is a sophomore-level computer science course created by Adrienne Bloss, a former colleague. Bloss's overall goals for the course are to have students learn, adapt, and apply sorting and searching algorithms that work with large, messy data sets. Bloss decided to design her course using our particular region, southwestern Virginia, and she asks students to work with real-life data from a regional commission that collects employment data. She chose to break the course into three case studies, using three different sets of data each time and bringing in new algorithms, theories, and techniques with each new set (see Table 3.8) (A. Bloss, personal communication, June 23, 2008).

In contrast to Olin, each of the case studies Bloss uses requires a formal assignment. This is important because it brings into play the learning cycle described by Zull (2002) in the previous chapter. As students are

TABLE 3.8
**Course Design Using Case Studies: Computer Science**

| *Case Study* | *Summary* |
|---|---|
| No. 1 | Students were provided with data sets dealing with the size of the employers in the region. Through reading, discussion, lecture, and trial and error, students learned about various models for sorting and searching algorithms. Once they'd had their initial introductions to the various models and techniques, students were asked to choose the searching and sorting model they felt would work best with this particular data. They were then asked to rationalize their choice, using what they'd learned from the course thus far. |
| No. 2 | Students examined a second data set having to do with employer growth (or shrinkage) over time. They studied more algorithms, more discussions, and more explorations, then were required, again, to choose and provide the rationalization for the best algorithm for the situation. |
| No. 3 | Students had access to a third data set, this time not only of employers but of employment fields. Here again, they learned more algorithms, more theory, and more techniques. The students discussed the greater complexities of these data sets and were set to work. |

encountering course material, they are constantly thinking about how this material applies to the work they will do. As a result, their learning is deepened. Even better, that course material is linked to life beyond the classroom. This is valuable because it reminds students that what they are learning has a purpose beyond the usual test-taking games they are forced to endure in our age of standardization. Also, the data sets Bloss uses are likely messy and unpredictable. Even the instructor doesn't know what the answers will turn out to be; as such, students are getting practice with the kind of work they'll be doing once they graduate and won't be able to look in the back of the book for the perfectly calculated answer.

Finally, Bloss's approach is effective because as the case studies progress, they become more complicated. The first data set is relatively static. The second tracks movement over time. The third also tracks movement but with a larger and messier data set involving not only finite employers but also fields of employment. This means that students must make some decisions about how parameters will be set, how terms are to be defined, and about which business falls into what category. Bloss complicates this even further by removing herself from the equation. The first case study is resolved with heavy instructor involvement. The second is worked on collaboratively, with students helping one another. For the third case study, students must do their work individually.

One final example of the case study approach comes from mathematician Paul Olsen, who teaches a general education mathematics course themed around issues of gambling. By the end of the semester Olsen wants his students to be able to do the following:

1. Calculate or predict odd probabilities, expected values, and house edges for events dealing with games of chance.
2. Explain in written (and mathematical) form the various concepts of the course.
3. Articulate and compare the concepts of decision analysis and mold these criteria into one's own personality, morals, or ethics.
4. Decide when gambling is okay and when gambling is problematic.

Olsen's course doesn't require a textbook; most of the concepts are presented to the students through lectures and discussions, although some are also developed through interactions with guest speakers, including counselors with Gamblers Anonymous, and from field trips, including a visit to a nearby racetrack. Olsen also brings into play what he refers to as "game by game" discussion and analysis using the following for case studies (P. Olsen, personal communication, January 8, 2014):

- lotteries, including a comparison of lotteries in the United States, Europe, and Asia
- table games (roulette, craps, etc.)
- poker games (note the plural here: Do different nuances in the rules lead to different results?)
- bridge
- horse racing
- business expansion
- life insurance

I've included Olsen's course for a number of reasons. First, unlike the courses designed by Olin and Bloss, each of which uses only three extended case studies, Olsen has chosen to include seven shorter studies. Obviously, there are pluses and minuses to either option. Fewer studies allows more depth, whereas more variety is less likely to cause boredom and increases the odds of connecting with student interests. The important thing to remember is that there are options; there is no perfect number of case studies that guarantees success in a course. Each of us has to look at our fields, our course content, how that content connects with life beyond the classroom, and go from there.

Second, I like how Olsen's last two case studies—business expansion and life insurance—expand traditional thinking about what is and isn't gambling. I think this is important because it reinforces the idea that what we're doing in the classroom is not some esoteric indulgence of the academic mind but substance intimately connected to daily life. This is key to designing a good course. All of us believe deeply that our fields matter, that students' lives are richer and more thoughtful for knowing the content, ideas, and methodologies of our fields. And I'd say we're right. But I'd also say that a lot of the time we do a lousy job of making that connection apparent to our students. Oh, sure, every once in a while we throw in a real-life anecdote or make a point about some event in the daily news, but in the context of two 90-minute lectures a week in a 14-week semester, those 5 or 10 minutes of cultural reference don't add up to much. I think it's incumbent on us to stress to our students how our courses and their content matter to them, really matter. And we need to do this in substantive ways.

Third, and to end this section on a lighter note, I included Olsen's course simply because it looks like so much fun: Seriously, who wouldn't want to take this class? In the end, it's important to remember that we all find a certain joy in our fields. Why not find a way to bring that joy into our course designs?

## *Project-Based Learning*

The project-based learning approach (sometimes also referred to as problem-based learning) is similar to the case study approach in the constant emphasis on the connection between course concepts and the world beyond the classroom. It differs from the case study approach in that project-based learning generally spends the entire semester focusing on a single, very large and complex problem, constantly applying course material to the resolution of that problem.

For example, I teach a general education senior capstone course titled Communicating the Liberal Arts. I designed this course when I noticed a trend at my institution: Although my college had done an excellent job revising its general education curriculum, economic pressures and messages from mass media made many of our students feel that the liberal education side of their coursework was a distraction from their major, despite reams of evidence that employers are looking for the exact skills obtained from a liberal arts education.

The purpose of my course was to respond to this problem. The students' final project was to design a campaign to counter the views held by their peers across campus, making an argument, both rhetorical and action based, for the value of the liberal arts. Their final project could include anything from posters to T-shirts to computer apps to activities fairs. The only requirements were that these campaigns include the best research concerning the role of a liberal arts education in today's world; invoke best practices in engaged learning as understood by cognitive neuroscientists and developmental psychologists; and that students design, conduct, and use the results from a survey of a particular population with a stake in the general education debate.

One distinguishing feature of the projects in a project-based course is that they are large and comprehensive. In the end, the student-designed campaigns in this particular course count for 50% of the final grade. I want to get the students' attention. I want them to know that this project matters—they can't just attend the course, take a couple of exams, and pass.

Another distinguishing feature of these projects is that students are working on them almost from the first week of the course. When, early on, we read various definitions of *liberal education* and various arguments for its value, students are prompted to think about their own projects and the particular audiences they might work with: How might these audiences respond to the articles and books we're reading? When we then begin to read psychological material about how people learn and make important decisions, students retire to their collaborative groups and brainstorm practices that may help to bring their message to their audiences. When we discuss survey methods, they then design and administer surveys. And so on.

All semester, every reading, every discussion, every in-class activity, every lecture is geared toward the final project. This is essential because it contextualizes the course content, providing students with a clear sense of its relevance and meaning. This differs greatly from our traditional classes, where often the instructor's implicit message is "Trust me. Some day—maybe this semester, maybe after you graduate—you'll come to see how important this stuff is." In a project-based course, this relevance is always in the foreground, applied constantly. As a result, students' learning is deepened, and they're more likely to leave the course remembering the material.

This sort of extended practice in problem-solving also contributes to students' sense of authority. After having worked on a complex, long-term project like this with all its ups and downs, students will feel more prepared, more qualified, and more confident confronting the same sorts of tasks in a postgraduate environment, either at work or as citizens in a fairly messed-up world.

One can see how this sort of project-based approach could easily be adapted to a number of different courses. Students taking a computer science course could have an overarching project they work on all semester long; students in a studio arts course could be asked to assemble a portfolio exploring representations of gender. My colleague in physics has designed a junior-level theory course in which he presents students in the first week with an array of the big questions that drive his field, asks them each to choose one, and then has them work on that question all semester long, constantly applying their reading, research, discussions, and lectures toward a final solution that they then present to the rest of the class.

One could also see how these sorts of problem/project-based learning structures could hook into the community around the university. Part of the reason students tend to engage in my course on advocating for the liberal arts is that they soon understand that this is a real problem, not just some exercise in a textbook. Are there ways, then, that your course might actually go out into the neighborhoods and rivers and streams around the college, collect real data, and use that data to address real problems?

In the Reacting to the Past (2017) project at Barnard College, instructors set up elaborate games that require students to master course content in order to address major questions or solve large problems at key turning points in a variety of fields: the trial of Galileo, the ratification of the U.S. Constitution, India on the eve of independence, the rise of Darwin and naturalism, and so on. Although some faculty resist the word "game," they're missing the point. The purpose of approaches like this is to bring the major questions of the field into play, foregrounding for students the debates and histories and complexities that faculty often take for granted. As a result, with this sort of approach, students are less likely to see course content as a series of discrete facts, whose sole use is to be memorized for the exam. Rather, they come to understand the systems of thinking that help scholars organize this information and understand why this information matters. In short, these games help students move beyond superficial learning toward expertise. What more could we want?

---

### Designing Your Course: Step 7

1. All our fields matter, all our fields strive to solve some of the complex issues of the day. Take a moment and brainstorm a list of real-world issues, questions, or problems related to your field.
2. Next, brainstorm a list of the major questions in your field. What are the debates that scholars have had for years? What are some of the debates you anticipate them having in the next few years as a result of changes in the field or the world?
3. Now examine these two lists. Recognizing that you're simply exploring possibilities, take a moment to draw up two to three project-based models that might work for your course and your goals. In each rough draft, explore these components:
   - What question or questions might drive the course?
   - What content or skills would be included to provide students with the ability to address this problem or question?
   - What might the final project in this project-based course look like?
4. Set these drafts aside, keeping them in mind as one possible approach for structuring the overall arc of your course.

# INTERMISSION

## Putting It All Together: Part One

The brain, we know, can only handle so much information at once. Neuroscientists differ, but most agree that working memory can only manage between three and seven items at any given time.

Considering how much material we've already covered, it's important to take a moment and take stock of where you are thus far in the course design process. That in mind, I'd like you to work through the steps presented here. Remember that as with everything else we're doing here, this is just a draft. Revisions can occur later; indeed, more often than not, revisions *will* occur as we cover more material and our understanding of course design expands. This recursiveness is a good sign, as it means that our brains are moving beyond the lockstep approach we so often take toward creating our courses. In other words, as we revise, refine, and reshape our work, we're often deepening our thinking, moving beyond the most obvious ideas toward approaches that really match the needs of our students and our own skills and interests.

I want to make one minor recommendation. Often for this stage it helps to shift the medium you're working in. In other words, if thus far you've been working on your computer, move now to pen and paper; if you've been working with pen and paper, perhaps use a marker on a whiteboard. Shifting the medium in this way often helps you get a fresh perspective so you can see your work from a new angle.

Step 1: Look at the drafts of the goals you created in chapter 2:

- At first glance, do any obvious revisions leap out at you? If so, implement those changes now. If you find yourself stuck at this stage, it might help to peruse Krathwohl's (2002) taxonomy.
- Remember the three keys to creating effective goals:
  - They require students to engage actively with course content in authoritative ways.

- ◦ They provide measurable evidence of what students have or haven't achieved.
- ◦ They engage students on a level that enacts our best hopes for them.

Step 2: Keeping those goals in mind, consider the various possible structures you came up with in chapter 3, such as

- typological structures (chapter 3, pp. 45–54): *categorical, chronological, methodological, theoretical,* and *use*;
- problem-based or case study structures (chapter 3, 55–59); and.
- goals-based structures (chapter 3, pp. 60–62).

Step 3: Choose a single structure that seems to work well with your goals, effectively communicates key knowledge to students in a way that makes sense to someone less familiar with the field, and appeals to you.

Step 4: If necessary:

- Make revisions to the organization or order of your chosen structure.
- Flesh out the contents or ideas of your structure.
- Revise your goals to better match your structure.

Step 5: Set all this aside for now.

# 4

# CREATING WICKED
# ASSIGNMENTS

The English department at my college has an excellent course, a senior seminar in which the same group of students work together all year. The course is 6 hours per week and only counts as a single credit despite its double requirement. Over the duration of 2 semesters, the students in this class struggle, suffer, fail, succeed, bond, grow, struggle, succeed, grow, grow, and grow. Part of the dynamic is simply the safe space created by having the same 15 students work together for 9 months. The real key to the course, however, lies in what is required of them. The first day, 3 students each bring an individually crafted bibliography on *Beowulf* and present their own ideas. Then on the second day, 3 other students make the same kind of presentation on Chaucer, the third day is *Sir Gawain and the Green Knight,* and so on. The instructor for the course meets with the students before their presentations, hears an initial description of their ideas, prods and gives advice, and maybe offers a source or two. But when it comes to the actual presentation, the students must assume absolute accountability for their work. There is no safety net. In other words, this is not one of those situations where the student's presentation is a precursor to more meaningful comments by the professor or where the professor is waiting in the wings ready to swoop in and bring everything to a tidy conclusion if something goes wrong. Only the student's words count.

What's astounding about this class is how it changes the students. By being forced to take responsibility for their own learning, the students grow tremendously, almost to the point that they are unrecognizable by the end of the year; the light in their eyes is just that much different.

The point here is one that I've made before, and will undoubtedly make again. There is really only one way for people to gain authority: They must assume it, repeatedly and often. Sometimes this occurs in small situations that don't count for very much, sometimes in major situations that count a great deal. Sometimes they fail, sometimes they succeed. That sense that one is capable of engaging in complex problem-solving can only come from solving complex problems. This is explored in more detail in this and the next two chapters, first by examining assignment and exam design in a wicked context and then by reviewing the day-to-day teaching techniques that help instructors nurture authority in their students.

## Contexts of Uncertainty

Randy Bass (2014), who runs a pedagogical incubator at Georgetown University, once made the argument that high-impact practices succeed because, among other things, they "offer the opportunity to integrate, synthesize, and make meaning," pushing students to "make decisions in the midst of uncertainty." Because our goal here is to have the same kind of impact as these high-impact practices, I am adopting Bass's language as we move forward. Whatever else the assignments and exam questions we design in the following pages achieve, they must ask students to

- *make meaning*, that is, construct new ideas or solutions to problems, as well as new understandings of those problems and their causes; alternatively, they may ask students to look forward into the future and make predications based on their learning;
- *integrate*, that is, foreground useful connections among seemingly disparate areas of thought, with the goal of adapting problem-solving methodologies from one context to another;
- *synthesize*, similar to making meaning in that students must bring together ideas to create a new understanding of a problem or a solution to that problem; and
- *make decisions*, or take action, based on their thinking as they make meaning, integrate, and synthesize.

Furthermore, students should do these things whenever possible

- *in contexts of uncertainty.*

If anything, this last idea is the most important; if our goal is prepare students for a real world filled with complex problems, we need to begin by bringing that complexity into our classrooms. If we're doing our jobs correctly, there will be no answers at the back of the book, no websites that can be skimmed for easy solutions. Students will be required to draw from a variety of ideas and methodologies, essentially making it up as they go along—and I mean that in a positive way!

Given our criteria for success, perhaps it is useful to examine more traditional modes of assignments to see how they measure up. Consider, for instance, the traditional academic writing assignment. As I've written elsewhere (Hanstedt, 2012), every rhetorical situation has three basic components: the speaker or writer, the topic, and the audience that is reading or listening. Change one of these elements, and the style, tone, and content of the communication will change. So a student writing an e-mail to a friend about a final exam will sound very different when that same student writes to a friend about a party, which will sound very different when the student writes to the professor about the final exam (we've all received those e-mails).

When we think of traditional writing assignments, the rhetorical situation usually plays out as illustrated in Figure 4.1. In terms of authority, what's noteworthy here is that it all lies with the professor. The professor has been studying a topic for years and has the grade book and all the power it carries with it to shape not only a student's grade in the course but the direction of his or her future. The student, on the other hand, has virtually no power, having been in the course for 10, maybe 12 weeks before receiving the final assignment. The student knows the course content only as a consequence of what has been assigned by the professor, said by the professor in lecture, or stated in the context of a discussion controlled by the professor.

For all practical purposes, then, the rhetorical triangle should look like Figure 4.2.

**Figure 4.1.** Traditional academic assignments.

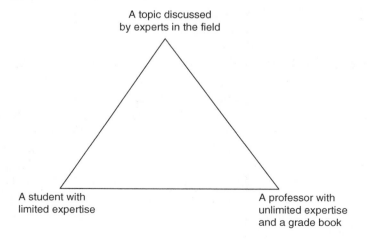

A topic discussed
by experts in the field

A student with
limited expertise

A professor with
unlimited expertise
and a grade book

**Figure 4.2.** Traditional writing assignments in terms of authority.

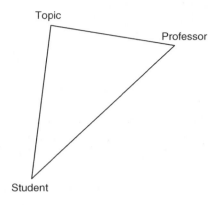

As one of my colleagues observed, the triangle in Figure 4.2 already looks so much like a dagger that you might as put a handle on it. In this situation, the student is staring up at the professor and the topic, essentially helpless at the bottom of a long, steep hill. For all but our best students, the rhetorical challenges of this situation are tremendous. Many of them try to assume authority by drafting jargon-laden prose that often escapes their control; others gloss over key concepts, working (accurately) with the assumption that their audience—the professor—already knows this stuff; and still others simply skim outside sources until they've found so many quotations to drop into their papers that we never actually learn what they are thinking, much less see them achieve any ownership of the topic.

With all this in mind, it's perhaps clear that what we want is to create some sort of rhetorical situation where students must assume authority for their papers, taking responsibility for their ideas and constructing new understandings of a text, a theorem, or a political dilemma. At moments like this, I remember my own experiences in graduate school and my attempts to gain expertise in the field of Victorian literature. I had to take three weekend-long qualifying exams before I could write my dissertation. Then I had to defend those exams in front of professors in my department. You would think that these kinds of experiences would cause a person to make sense of a field. But as many professors I've spoken to agree, the point when I really became the master of this content was when I first stepped into a classroom full of undergraduates. Then it was just me. Could I explain the relevance of imagination in the Romantic era? Could I construct a cohesive, intelligible narrative of the evolution of Victorian thought? At that point—and only at that point—did I begin to master the material. Faced with an audience of less-informed people, I became the authority.

**Figure 4.3.** Reinvisioning the rhetorical triangle to increase student authority.

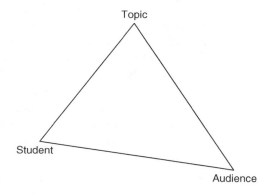

Perhaps, then, if we want our students to assume authority, the rhetorical triangle should be more along the lines of that shown in Figure 4.3. In this situation, the student is more knowledgeable than the audience. As a consequence, he or she must take on the responsibility of explaining everything to the audience without glossing over complicated concepts, using the rationalization that "the professor already knows this," or citing class discussion as an official source. Because students can't assume their audiences have any more than a basic understanding of the material being covered, outside sources must be introduced and summarized carefully. Similarly, all quotations must be analyzed by the student, woven into the language and argument of the student's paper in ways that someone who knows nothing about the topic will be able to follow. Students tend to assume that quotations speak for themselves. They don't. They must always be tied in to the larger argument in meaningful ways. In other words, changing the audience of a paper from the implied professor to an explicitly less familiar reader pushes our students to do all the things we've been trying to get them to do: explain their ideas, provide context, analyze carefully, and avoid oversimplified assumptions about what is and is not obvious.

This sort of rhetorical reconstruction pushes students to assume authority. For example, a biology professor I worked with in Delaware designed an assignment for her first-year seminar on emerging infectious diseases that asked students to

> create an informational pamphlet on an emerging infectious disease, pitched to PTO [Parent-Teacher Organization] parents. Include causative agent and vector, threat to local population, and possible measures to reduce risk. (K. Curran, personal communication, January 8, 2014)

The beauty of an assignment like this is that it requires students to tackle and understand some complex terms (*causative agent* and *vector*) as well as master some challenging methodologies (e.g., determining risk for a particular geographical area), and then explain it to an audience that didn't take the course, in language the audience will understand. In other words, the thinking in this course is still high; the expectations of the assignment are not in any way watered down from what they would be in a traditional paper. But because students have to translate this complex material to a less-informed audience, they are forced to own the material in ways they otherwise would not. They must find their own language to explain these ideas. They must make sense of the content for themselves. They must make meaning.

In another example from a required general education course on Western civilization, the students are told,

> You are running for Congress. In an address to your potential constituents explain how the political, religious, economic, or social problems in Rome might inform policy in an American context.

Here again we have complex topics the student needs to understand before being able to explain it to others. There is no room for glossing or skating over topics, relying on the professor's knowledge. There is no professor here, just potential voters, many of whom likely know very little about economic practices in ancient Rome.

It is worth noting that this example also asks students to apply course content to a new setting by integrating information and making meaning: How do Roman social problems relate to our world today? How might these problems help us understand the underlying causes of our issues? What solutions might we glean from the Romans? How might these solutions need to be adapted? In situations like these, there are no perfect answers. Certainty does not exist. Students have to think for themselves, analyze by themselves, create by themselves.

The following is an example from Genelle Gertz of Washington and Lee University, drawn from her class on metaphysical poetry:

> You have been invited to lecture to two separate audiences on John Donne. You are asked to deliver a sermon to a Christian congregation (you can specify an exact one if you wish) on spiritual principles in John Donne's poetry. Then the next day you address a local atheist group on John Donne's religious poetry. Provide a close reading of at least one poem and draw upon relevant sources in our reading.

Gertz's instructions continue:

> Just as John Donne inhabited different roles throughout his life, and changed for different audiences, so too, you inhabit different perspectives in this assignment. How might Donne's poetry speak to a church congregation? Your church audience is united by its faith, but it likely has a range of educational backgrounds and ages. Only a few will have been English majors. Contrastingly, how will you address a group of nonbelievers on the same subject? What will you emphasize in this setting that you might not have in the previous one? (G. Gertz, personal communication, October 3, 2013)

Gertz has complicated her students' task by giving them not one but two audiences they need to consider. Here again, the students have to own the content to be able to explain it. But even better, they become rhetorically nimble with that content, recognizing how meaning is made differently for different people. This is a challenging assignment to be sure, but completely appropriate for an advanced course in the field.

All three of these examples involve more or less general audiences—the voting populace, a group of parents, and people who attend church and people who don't. But as Danielewizc and Jack have pointed out, slightly more focused audiences might also be appropriate for academic assignments. They suggest writing to "nonspecialists," a group they define as generally knowledgeable in a discipline without necessarily being an expert (J. Danielewizc & J. Jack, personal communication, February 13, 2009). For instance, students enrolled in a course in nutrition might be given the following assignment:

> The New York state government has created a council to develop a list of recommendations regarding the lifestyles of primary school age children. As the nutritionist on the council, your job is to choose a region, examine its population, and construct an appropriate menu for breakfast, providing a carefully researched rationale that takes into consideration all the relevant components of our work this semester.

In this case, although the menu is being prepared for the general public, the rationale and all the logic, evidence, and analysis it contains is pitched to the other members of the council, who, although knowledgeable generally about child health, may not be nutritionists. Some faculty prefer this type of audience, as it pushes students toward a slightly more formal approach, often creating a tone that faculty feel is more appropriate for an academic or professional setting. Nonetheless, the assignment still requires students to adopt a degree of authority; they must still define terms, clarify relevant criteria, carefully examine their logic. Further, because each student chooses a different region of the state and consequently a different population, he or she is working in a setting of uncertainty because what applies to one region might not apply to another. Students must each find their own way.

The following is another example of an authoritative assignment pitched to nonspecialists, designed for an advanced Spanish course in South American culture:

> You are part of a medical organization about to expand into Bolivia. Your job is to explain to the members of your team some of the cultural and linguistic challenges they might encounter in the region. In order to give your paper focus, concentrate on a particular health issue, indigenous culture, or geographic location.

Here again, the students are placed in the role of expert. They are the ones who know, who must explain. Their audience, although generally well informed, lacks their specific knowledge. As a result, the students must assume authority and become the people whose knowledge allows them to look into the future and make some predictions about what will occur, not only in terms of general language and culture but relative to matters of health or region or a particular native group. I particularly like this model because it replicates the kinds of applied work a student of modern languages might take on after graduation. Although some portion of any graduating class majoring in a language might end up teaching, many more students will find themselves working in industry, business, health care, or social services, where their knowledge of language and culture is only part of the equation; in other words, they're going to have to feel their way through new challenges on an almost daily basis.

---

### Designing Your Course: Step 8

1. Take a moment and go back to the course you are working with. Brainstorm a list of general population audiences that might have an interest in the content, ideas, and methodology of your course. Keep in mind that brainstorming means putting down every idea that comes into your head. Do not edit or censor at this stage; there will be plenty of time for that later.
2. Still thinking about this course, brainstorm a list of nonspecialist audiences who might be interested in your course content and ideas, that is, audiences that are informed in general about your discipline or field of study but who likely won't have particular knowledge of the nuances of your course topic.
3. Set these two lists aside until the end of this chapter.

## Beyond Paper Assignments

What if you're in a field where paper assignments aren't necessarily the norm? Or what if the students at your institution aren't particularly inspired by writing assignments, even nontraditional ones? What if you've seen enough papers to last you a lifetime, and you're just looking for something new?

### Oral Presentations

Almost everything we're talking about here can easily be shifted to other genres and disciplines. Consider, for instance, a class where the major requirement is an oral presentation. Normally this means a student who has researched a topic related to the course stands up and gives a talk to a group of other students who've also researched a topic related to the course. Although this sort of assignment can work well in some situations—for example, when the students listening are particularly polite, or the student speaking has chosen a topic that has some intrinsic appeal to the audience— very often, presentations like this have an arbitrary, meaningless feel to them: The students are not doing this because it truly matters but because it's expected.

What happens, though, if we change the implied audience for a presentation to a group of people who really don't know much about the topic and have some intrinsic interest in it? It's possible, in other words, to reconstruct the rhetorical context so that the speaker must take authority over the spoken content and what's being discussed really matters. I'm reminded of a workshop I did years ago where, as we were discussing alternative assignments, a woman in the back of the room suddenly shouted, "Oh!" I stopped what I was doing, and we all looked at her, wondering if she'd had a heart attack. She hadn't. What she'd had was an epiphany. "I teach gender studies," she told us. "And every semester I have students give talks on male gender roles. And every semester it's the same old thing, the choir preaching to the choir. What if—" and here she paused, for she had our attention now, "instead of having them talk to the class, I had them pretend they were talking to a group of 12-year-old boys?" And then everyone in the room said, "Oh!" Because we got it now too. In the first scenario, student talking to students, nothing really matters. In the second scenario, students talking to tween boys who are about to begin their own exploration of the varying models of maleness, everything matters. The latter speech, that talk, is an opportunity to change individual lives, social expectations, and society as a whole. Suddenly presentations that had felt like meaningless academic exercises felt very real, very significant, and very powerful.

Frankly, at moments like this the whole issue of authority doesn't really seem very important in comparison to our desire to make learning powerful and purposeful. But that's the point: By shifting rhetorical focus, we're creating a situation that transcends mere academia by putting students in challenging situations where things matter. Kind of like life.

## Comprehensive Projects

The following instructions are from another assignment, developed by Zach Adams, formerly of Wesley College. They come from the major project for a first-year seminar on art and community murals:

> Create a proposal for a local public mural in the Dover area for possible grant/funding applications. Include and prepare a rationale for a description of the project, the long-term goals for community impact, several means of creating community input and involvement, and a budget. (Z. Adams, personal communication, January 8, 2014)

There's so much to like about this assignment. Most obviously, it asks students to assume authority in a very real way: They are working in the community now with real people, a real goal, and a real impact. This matters. The students must think about the needs of the Dover community so they can develop long-term goals for their project, learn about the various means of gathering community input for an art project, evaluate those methods, choose and rationalize an appropriate approach, conceptualize and rationalize an art project that would meet those needs, and develop a budget and a rationale. In other words, this project asks students to integrate multiple disciplines (art, sociology, mathematics), synthesize complex information from multiple sources, make meaning in the form of a new community mural, and do all this in a situation that has better and worse answers—but no certainty.

## Quantitative Reasoning

That mathematics plays a role in Adams's assignment is also important for several reasons. First of all, for most of our students, quantitative reasoning is usually going to matter in an applied way; that is, students will use it in their work for a nonprofit, a web design firm, or a car rental agency. Math matters, and this assignment makes that starkly clear to a group of first-year art students who at first may see mathematics as unnecessary. The students who take this first-year seminar will learn the value of mathematics to their career goals and may, as a result, approach any required mathematics courses with a higher degree of intrinsic motivation.

Second, I like that this assignment asks students to write about mathematics. They can't simply put the numbers down and walk away. This is important, because as a lot of faculty who regularly teach quantitative reasoning will tell you, one of the biggest challenges they face is getting students to actually understand the ideas behind mathematical formulas. Students can do the math, but when the situation or the context changes, these same students find themselves at a loss; for example, how do they reconfigure a one-dimensional equation on a two-dimensional graph? Asking students to actually write about what they're doing, to justify and explain their quantitative approaches, helps shift students' roles from passive to authoritative (Bahls, 2012).

Consider, for instance, an assignment designed by Patrick Bahls (2012), in which, as students go through the semester and learn various concepts, they write a mathematics textbook for other students, providing "explanations of key course concepts as well as visual aids, examples, and exercises as appropriate" (p. 110). Think about the complexity of this; to explain key concepts, students must first thoroughly understand those concepts, then find the language to articulate those concepts to someone who is unfamiliar with them. To develop visual aids, students must shift their thinking from numbers and words to images, which requires a complex cognitive translation not only of language but also the medium. To develop examples and exercises, students must step beyond what they've learned in the textbook and through discussion and lecture and create something entirely new, scaling examples and exercises in a developmental way to move their readers gradually from complete ignorance to understanding. Recalling Krathwohl's (2002) taxonomy, clearly this project has students spending a great deal of time on the far right-hand side of the taxonomy, engaging in cognitively challenging acts. Although Bahls constructs this as a semester-long project (students do extensive and impressive work brainstorming, drafting, responding, and so on), he makes the point that it could easily be scaled back into a series of study guides or even *CliffNotes*.

A final quantitative example, drawn from the legendary physics professor Thomas Knorr at Wheeling Jesuit University, concerns a midlevel lab for physics majors (S. Vargas, personal communication, June 15, 2016). Knorr assigned each of his students a wicked problem they were required to solve completely on their own. For example, one student was asked to develop a method for calculating the ratio of buildings to lawns on campus, another was asked to calculate the number of blades of grass on campus, and another, the volume of water flowing in a nearby stream. In each case, students were to develop a method for determining the answer, provide their calculations, and provide a final number. They had absolutely no supervision, although Knorr was available to answer questions and offer support, which was good, because even his cohort of very good physics majors found themselves struggling—at least at first. There were no formulas for these problems, no answers at the back of the textbook. The Internet didn't exist then, but even if it had, it wouldn't have helped. Eventually, though, his students learned to calm down, think about various problems they'd dealt with in the past, and think about how they might adapt the methods they used to solve those problems to the current issue. They experimented. They bombed. Then they experimented again, eventually finding a fingerhold, then a foothold, and then a solution. Maybe it was not a perfect solution, maybe not the solution an experienced physicist would have found, but that wasn't the point. The goal here was to place students in situations that replicated the kind of work real physicists do in the lab. Not telling them, "Here's a problem, here's a protocol, now plug in the numbers," but rather, "Here's a problem. Now what?"

We can tell this is an authoritative assignment because it makes no difference whatsoever that the audience for the final project is the professor. After all, in cases like these, he is the uninformed audience. As one former student put it, "What I realized much much later is that it wasn't about coming up with a correct answer. (Like Knorr actually knew the volume of dirt?)" (M. Carigen, personal communication, June 21, 2016).

Perhaps most important here are the results, that is, the students Knorr produced. As one of them told me, "In hindsight I realize Dr. Knorr was creating great problem solvers. He never gave a lab that was straightforward. By the end of the semester you were just ready for the impossible and were willing to stay up all night to make it possible" (S. Vargas, personal communication, June 21, 2016).

## Blended Assignments, Poster Projects, and Real-World Audiences

It's worth noting that although all these projects are constructed as hypothetical—in other words, students aren't literally speaking to 12-year-old boys or writing to first-year math students—there's nothing that says they couldn't be realistic. For years, the major first-year writing exercise at the University of Vermont was to have each year's students construct essays and readings for next year's freshmen. Sometimes the shift to a real audience is just what a project needs to push students further into authority. Consider, for instance, my experiences teaching Composition Theory and Practice, a course that teaches people how to teach writing. In early iterations of the syllabus, the final project was fairly standard: Students were asked to choose a population with literacy needs, such as high school seniors preparing for college, create a course of study for those students, and write a rationale explaining the choices they'd made as they completed the project.

On the face of it, this is a fairly authoritative assignment. Students are looking at a wicked problem (teaching is always a wicked problem) and constructing new ideas for approaching it. Certainly, some of the projects I was given were pretty good, but even the better ones were—how can I say this—powerfully mundane? Students were clearly doing what was expected of them, but there wasn't a lot of energy in their work. They achieved the desired ends, but there was no flair, no focus, no indication that students would leave the class and move into the world with a sense of urgency. And when you're dealing with issues of language, identity, and power, this is rather troubling.

It also bothered me—and this is a trend that I see often in matters of authority—that the better projects almost inevitably came from the better students. When I asked students to engage in this authoritative task, the students who already had a sense of their intellectual and academic authority were fine, but those who did not—the B and C students, the nontraditional students, and the first-generation students—struggled.

This is not good. We are educators after all. Our goal is to educate—everyone. If we find ourselves in a situation where the best stay the best and the less stay the less, then chances are we're not educating, we're simply affirming the status quo. I don't know about anyone else, but I didn't suffer through seven years of graduate school so that I could leave things exactly the way I found them.

What I eventually did, in a moment of frustration, was shift the syllabus project from a completely written assignment to a blended assignment, one that combined mediums. The first part of the project—the construction of a course of study for a particular population—became a poster presentation (see Appendix A). What's more, this poster presentation occurred in the student center, just outside the dining hall over the lunch hour. Further, I advertised it on the campus website. My students were expected to show up looking professional, ready to explain the choices they'd made while designing their courses to anyone who stopped by. And people did stop by: friends, classmates, professors, even the college president. And they asked questions. I remember one group that designed an entire syllabus around digital literacies, arguing that this was a great way to reach disengaged high schoolers. A professor from the computer science program, known for his intelligence and his no-nonsense approach in the classroom, came to the session and read the group's poster. Once he finished, he proceeded to grill the students, hammering them with question after question for almost 20 minutes. Standing back, I felt nervous for the group. They'd only been in my class for 13 weeks after all and were still learning this stuff. Once the professor left and the session was over, I checked in with the students. "That looked a little rough," I said. "No," they replied, almost in unison. "It was fantastic. He really cared!"

Consequently, the students cared. In the weeks running up to the presentations, students would cluster at the end of class, swapping ideas and figuring out when to meet. I'd see groups in the commons late in the afternoon, sipping coffee and huddling over their laptops. Even the individual rationales students wrote for their projects had more energy, were more engaged and engaging. I saw students from all levels develop as thinkers and writers. Presenting students with real audiences in real situations sharpens even more that sense of urgency that can lead to authority: This is not a drill, not some meaningless exercise. What they're learning in this class and the things they do in this class matter beyond the end of the semester.

## *Videos and Other Digital Media*

Another approach that invokes real-world audiences is video assignments. The basic premise here is that students create a short film incorporating some component of the course for an audience who would benefit from that content. For instance, I teach a first-year seminar on travel literature. In addition to reading and analyzing various travel narratives, my students also apply social theory and research on study abroad to our discussions. The final project for this course asks students to work in groups, sifting through the key ideas they've encountered over the course of the semester and developing a three- to seven-minute YouTube video for people about to study abroad, providing tips for a successful year (see Appendix B). The film must demonstrate complexity of thought about international and intercultural experiences and how they relate to learning and personal development. Students are encouraged always to consider their audience. Most college students won't watch a boring video, so humor is important, as is music of some sort. All films must include a list of sources that were used in preparation for the filming. Students are also required to write a carefully researched rationale that includes a clear thesis unifying the tips in the film, arguing the value of each tip, and contextualizing and analyzing all outside sources.

Key to the success of these films (several of which are good enough that I've actually sent them to our international education office) is the complexity of the task. Students have to evaluate multiple sources from multiple genres—some narrative, some academic, some theoretical, none of them particularly practical in a how-to kind of way—searching for ideas or the seeds of ideas that might apply to an undergraduate about to leave home for a long period of time. Then students must somehow synthesize these ideas into a cohesive structure, write a script, and edit it to a manageable size. Next, they must choose images to reinforce these ideas and music to fit the mood of the video as a whole and particular ideas more specifically. In doing this, they draft, receive feedback, revise, edit, draft, receive feedback, multiple times, continually deepening the level of thinking and the cohesiveness of the film as a whole. The project becomes very real, very meaningful—that is, very literally full of meaning. It matters.

The one thing students don't have to worry about as they create these projects is the technical aspect. The first time I had students create a video for a course, I brought in a specialist to talk about the various software and the nuances of film and sound editing. Halfway through his presentation, one of the students in the class who was a young poet and a notorious daydreamer, said, "Hey look! I made a movie." Then she turned her laptop around to show us that she had indeed created a short film, her first ever. Although claims that today's students are always and already digital natives have been overused, the fact is that most of the software for these kinds of projects is so available and so intuitive that it's difficult to form a group of students and not have at least two members already experienced in filmmaking.

The same can be said for website design programs and software. The Internet is full of cheap and reliable sites that allow students to design and launch their own websites. Because of this, there's no reason that this same assignment, or the assignment about literacy, creating a math book, or community murals, couldn't be refigured into a website assignment. Here again, the idea that what the students are creating is open to the world beyond the classroom gives the work more relevance and pushes students toward greater authority. After years of formalized and carefully controlled education, students are able to half listen to our words or skim over our comments fairly easily. The first time they create a Twitter account, blog, or a website related to a course and get retweeted or reposted or simply receive a comment from a real person not in the academic world is electrifying to them.

## Research

One thing I haven't discussed explicitly thus far is the role research plays in assignments of this kind. As academics, we tend to overassign research and research-driven papers, which is not surprising, given that for most of us this is the accepted genre. This can be a problem, though, because there are times when our goal is for our students to perform some of the basic functions of our discipline, such as reading carefully, summarizing effectively, performing a lab experiment, or creating a programming algorithm. Assigning these tasks while simultaneously requiring outside research may allow students to avoid demonstrating the skills we're really after, burying their own thinking in a blizzard of outside quotations and references.

Obviously, though, research and all it entails is a crucial skill for all of our students. The world is full of data, information of varying quality and relevance. With the 24-hour news cycle, the Internet, and social media, everyday citizens are bombarded with rumor pretending to be fact, innuendo based on nothingness, and very real and pertinent ideas that threaten to get lost in the avalanche of trivia. We need to create graduates who are capable of separating the real from the fake, the relevant from the trivial. They need practice, while still in college, in sifting through and evaluating the quality of varying sources and seeing the connections and disagreements that exist among these sources.

The problem from an authority-based standpoint is that often students writing traditional research papers are overreliant on their outside sources. Indeed, John Bean (2011) has coined the term *data dump* (p. 27) to describe student papers consisting almost entirely of quotations from outside sources. This approach allows writers to hedge their bets. They can't be wrong, their thinking goes, as long as everything they say is based on something someone else said. For most students, this feels like a much safer approach than actually throwing out some of their own ideas. Why risk that?

Very often, then, students who are asked to incorporate research into their work are never put into the position of having to make decisions in contexts of uncertainty. Which is fine, except for the fact that life is made up of uncertainty, and we want to prepare our graduates for life.

One effective response to this dilemma is illustrated nicely by a poster project designed by Diane Parham, a professor of occupational therapy at the University of New Mexico (D. Parham, personal communication, March 14, 2016; see Appendix C). In her graduate-level course on evidence-based practices, she requires a final culminating project in which students research and make presentations on a narrowly focused question. They might, for example, analyze tai chi versus balance training for the elderly or sensory integration intervention for children with autism. Each student must find a minimum of five scholarly articles and briefly justify the search strategy they used to locate those pieces. They must also summarize the findings of those pieces, explaining their relevance to the overall project.

All of which is well and good, but from an authority-based standpoint, Parham's next move is crucial. Students are expected to answer the question,

"So what? . . . In other words, now that you have studied these articles, how should their findings, all together, best be used to guide clinical practices with respect to your question?" Parham then presents her students with the following series of questions to help them as they construct a guide to evidence-based practice:

- What *specific* interventions in occupational therapy do these studies support or *not* support?
- Given the levels of evidence of these research studies, with how much confidence can you draw conclusions about practice from them?
- To which populations might findings from the studies be generalized or not generalized?
- If you were in clinical practice in an area related to your poster, how would your knowledge of these studies, taken all together, influence decisions you might make about using the intervention for particular people? Given our knowledge, is there any way you can identify who might be a good candidate versus not so good of a candidate for this intervention?
- How might the knowledge that you have gained be used to guide practice policies in the workplace or in public health?
- What gaps in knowledge exists, as related to your clinical question? What do we still *not* know that would be important to find out, in order to answer your clinical question? (D. Parham, personal communication, March 14, 2016)

Although some of these prompts allow a basic summary of the outside sources (the first, for instance), what's notable here is that most of the questions push students off the cliff of safe, reliable outside sources into the open air of uncertainty. How do we identify who is or isn't a good candidate for a particular intervention? How might this research lead to changes in public or workplace policies? What else do we need to understand as we move forward with work in these areas? All of these, to varying degrees, require students to make meaning, to go beyond the research and construct new understandings of a question. Indeed, even the first question about interventions could require some integration, as students might draw from other areas of study in the field to find interventions that would work relative to their research question.

The point here is that even when we require research, and we should require it periodically, there are ways to set students up to assume authority, explicitly saying, "The first half of your paper works to summarize and contextualize research; the second half of your paper should demonstrate your ability to take this information beyond what's already been said, to develop new solutions or ways of doing things."

### Signature Work

Just how empowering might such an approach be? Consider a professor I met at a workshop, who proposed a series of papers for a typical first-year transfer-level composition course at a community college. Karen Wong of Skyline College in San Bruno, California, has had a great deal of success working with underrepresented and underprepared students and wanted to develop a course that taught crucial skills like writing and quantitative reasoning while simultaneously developing in her students a meta awareness of the challenges they face in gaining a university education—as well as some of the ways they might overcome those challenges (K.E. Wong, personal communication, June 16, 2016).

The first assignment she gives students asks them to write their educational narrative, describing what contributed to or hindered their success. Clustering all of these narratives together allows the class as a whole to "ascertain patterns" of helps and hindrances. This in turn leads nicely into a data analysis assignment, wherein students produce a paper analyzing outcomes data for disproportionate impact, exploring possible explanations for this impact, and providing graphs to explain this impact to more general, less-informed audiences.

The next steps in the sequence involve researching and proposing solutions to these problems, ending in a pitch to a relevant audience, such as first-generation students, teachers, administrators, or Bill and Melinda Gates. "For instance," Wong said, "if their intent is to mentor first-generation students, they might design a YouTube video." Every pitch comes with an independently written rationale "explaining why they used that medium, and what informed what they included and how they addressed their audience—in short, the purpose, the audience, and the genre" (K.E. Wong, personal communication, June 16, 2016).

There's so much to like in this proposal. Writing, quantitative reasoning, meta learning that leads to solutions that might help not just the audience but the writers themselves, all in a context where students must take responsibility for their learning, where they're placed in a position of authority and where they're required to struggle with and understand the concepts they're dealing with to be able to explain those concepts to others.

In many ways this assignment mirrors much of the recent talk in educational circles concerning *signature work*, which, according the Association of American Colleges & Universities (2015), is a semester-long (at least) project in which a student uses cumulative knowledge to "pursue a significant project related to a problem she or he defines" (p. 2). Signature work can occur in capstone courses, undergraduate research, internships, or in the creation of an ePortfolio. The important criteria are first, that it's student led, dealing with unscripted (wicked) problems, and second, that it's cumulative. Indeed, most institutions tend to regard signature work as occurring in a student's later years, which makes sense as that allows students to accumulate knowledge and the skills necessary to tackle a complex problem—as well as, I would argue, the authority necessary to approach such complex problems.

Of course, if we want college seniors to tackle signature work, then we need to prepare them for that work throughout their college careers, starting as Wong does in first-year seminars. After all, done right, signature work tackles complex, messy problems. Addressing those problems requires not just high-order thinking but a strong sense of one's own capabilities, a willingness to take risks and dive in, asking questions and stepping back and thinking and trying and failing, and then trying again. This cannot be developed in a single course late in a student's career.

I find a great deal of reassurance in the fact that when I visit campuses or speak at conferences, inevitably members of the audience already have some pet essays and projects they assign that push students toward authority. For me this foregrounds the fact that this whole concept is not new—many of us already do it sporadically, occasionally, or even consistently. We already recognize that when we place students in positions of authority, where the problems aren't static or simple and there are no clear solutions, that's when they do some of their best work. The goal now is to find ways to do this more often and more deliberately. This leads us to the question of how we ask questions, or in other words, to authoritative exams.

But first, please take a moment to solidify some of your thinking about assignment design with the following exercise.

## Designing Your Course: Step 9

1. Take a moment and go back to the course goals you developed earlier in this book. Are there goals that lead easily to authoritative assignments? For instance, "By the end of the course, students will be able to construct a personal nutritional plan appropriate for their age, body type, and lifestyle" leads very nicely into an assignment where students do just that: Construct a personal nutritional plan. Do any of your goals similarly clearly lead to assignments? If so, skip ahead to number 3.

2. If none of your goals lead directly to assignment designs, look at each goal and ask yourself: What could students do that would provide evidence that they've achieved this goal? Answers could range from design an experiment to analyze an unfamiliar painting to give a speech at the United Nations to write an opinion piece for the newspaper. Make a list of all the possible actions students could perform that would convince you they have mastered that particular learning goal.

3. Now reexamine the lists you made earlier in this chapter of possible general and nonspecialist audiences that might have some interest in your course's content. Which audiences might be appropriate for the tasks you've found or listed in numbers 1 and 2 of this exercise?

4. Take a moment and think about genre: Is this task best performed in essay form, as an oral presentation, as a poster, as a video, in some sort of blended format?

5. Give yourself 10 minutes to brainstorm a list of all possible assignments you might develop for your goals in this course. Do not, at this point, exclude any options. For each possibility, include the audience and genre.

6. Set your brainstormed list aside, wait a couple of days, and come back to it when your head is clear. Then, choose an assignment (or two, or three) that you feel would benefit your students.

# 5

# CREATING
# AUTHORITATIVE EXAMS

Just to be clear about this: It is essential for our exams to test content knowledge and skill levels. Almost every exam we give should have some questions whose purpose is solely to determine whether the students have retained the information they've encountered in readings, discussions, labs, and lectures. Further, some portion of many exams will test whether students can apply a mathematical or chemical formula appropriately. As I have made clear in the early chapters of this book, the kinds of authority we seek to enrich in our students are directly the consequence of content and skill knowledge. We're not interested in lucky guesses or arrogance, which tend to favor the privileged. Our goal is to educate all our students.

That said, there's always room in an exam or quiz to test integration, synthesis, and meaning making. Similarly, it's possible to bring in some degree of uncertainty. This is particularly true, because as we've established, performing these higher end tasks generally requires mastery of a course's skills and content knowledge.

## Written Exams

Allow me to illustrate by using my own field, literature. One fairly standard testing protocol in literature classes involves identification and analysis. For example, on the final exam for my Victorian literature course, I include 10 quotations from works we've read and discussed. Often, these are key passages we've analyzed in class that provide insight into the era or a particular work. I ask students to choose 7 or 8 of the quotations and then give them the following instructions:

Identify the following quotations, in each case providing the author, the title, the context (who is speaking to whom and under what circumstance), and the thematic significance of the passage to the work as a whole and/or to the Victorian period.

There's a lot to be said for including these kinds of questions on an exam; clearly, this section tests students' basic knowledge: what are the major themes of the Victorian period? Of this book? Did you read this book enough to recognize the characters? Who wrote *Bleak House?* All good questions. And fair, too, to the extent that they reward students who: a) did the reading; and b) showed up for class. Excellent.

If this is all my exam does, though, I'm not sure I'm doing the students a favor. Because finally, questions about who wrote *Bleak House* or about finding themes only serve those students who are going to graduate school, plan on teaching, or like to show off at cocktail parties. This covers about a third of the graduates from my department. For the rest, what's really crucial in the study of literature is the ability to dig through thousands and thousands of words and somehow find what matters, somehow construct a meaningful understanding from a blizzard of data. This is a skill that will help them daily as they read the newspaper or listen to a political speech, but also professionally as they argue in the boardroom, listen to a client in social services, or even work with quantitative data, which often come with lots of meaningless detritus that needs to be set aside to get to what actually matters.

In other words, the work my students face after they graduate often won't consist of tame problems, where the answer is fixed, predetermined, or provided to you by the teacher for simple regurgitation. Rather, they'll be facing those wicked problems where the data are in flux, simple solutions are hard to come by, and what works one time doesn't work the next.

Perhaps, in addition to some of the traditional questions I usually give my students, I need to push them a further by including the following in an exam:

The following is a poem we did not cover in this class. Argue whether it is a Victorian poem, paying close attention to style and content.

Or:

The following is a poem we did not cover in this class, although it is from the Victorian era. Drawing from a list of authors we've read this semester, tell me who wrote it. Make your argument based on style and content.

Or:

> The following is a poem we did not cover in this class. What is it trying to argue or say? How do you know? Make your argument by citing particular words or passages, and analyzing their possible meanings carefully.

The first two options are quite good; both of them push students into uncertainty and ask them to apply what they've learned in new circumstances. Obviously, both questions require the basic skills we value in the study of literature; one can't answer them successfully without knowing the course material.

The third example takes all this a step further. What matters here is not the era or the authors or identification but that crucial skill of making meaning. What is this poem trying to say? Can you sift through these words and construct a cogent reading? This question focuses on the conceptual skills that drive our field and will be useful to students when they leave college.

Some might cry "No fair!" with a question like this; it's not even about the class or the Victorian era. Indeed, such a question doesn't play by the traditional rules of educational testing to which our students are accustomed. To this I offer two responses. First, it would be easy enough to alter the question so there is a direct link to the surface-level content of the course, for instance,

> The following is a poem we did not cover in class. What is the author trying to argue or say? How do you know? Make your argument by citing particular words or passages and analyzing their possible meanings carefully. Once you've done this, make an argument about whether this is a Victorian poem, basing your conclusions on style and content.

By asking students to determine if the poem is from the Victorian era, questions of fairness are somewhat appeased. Clearly, the question now comes back to the usual, standard purposes of the course, namely, learning about the Victorian era.

My second reply to those who fear that a question of this sort unfairly changes the rules will be addressed more thoroughly in chapter 7, but essentially boils down to this: We can test anything we want as long as we let students know beforehand that we'll be testing these things, and as long as we give students a fair chance to practice the skills we're after. Indeed, the more nonstandard our testing methods, the more necessary and ethical it is to make room in the course to allow students to practice. Having said that, the floodgates burst open. Consider the following examples:

Robert Browning and Gerard Manley Hopkins are in a bar getting drunk and talking about poetry. By the end of the night would they (a) end up arguing to the point of physical violence? or (b) end up in an eternal bromance? Base your answer on their stated views on poetry and on the poetry itself.

Or:

Argue the necessity of teaching Victorian literature (the content and the poetics) to premedical students. Provide a rationale for your argument with close and careful readings of at least three works we've discussed this semester.

Both these examples push students into contexts of uncertainty. The one about Browning and Hopkins has only 2 possible answers but 50 reasonable rationales. The same is true with the premed question: Who knows what works the students will choose or why? Here again, there is no correct answer; it's all about the students' ability to integrate thinking from one area into another, to make meaning in a new context. The second question doesn't even give the students the option of disagreeing. They must make the argument for poetry in a premed curriculum. Although some part of me feels a little guilty about that—Isn't choice generally a good thing?—a greater part of me recognizes the necessity of placing students in situations where they're not necessarily comfortable, of having them explore other ways of thinking and viewing the world.

Further, both questions require students to practice the fundamental skill of the field, that is, close and careful reading. The basics are not left behind, they're just being applied in different ways and contexts. Again, this is important because we never know when or where our students will be called on to use their skills, what jobs they'll take, what countries they'll live in, or where their lives will take them. We need to get them used to the idea that what they learn in one class, or even one field, might come in handy in a multitude of unpredictable settings.

Another nice thing about questions like these is that they're adaptable to pretty much every field. Instead of Browning and Hopkins, the first question might involve John Stuart Mill and Marx, Durkheim and Barthes, J.M.W. Turner and Mary Cassatt, or Aristotle and Yasmina Reza. The second question about the relevance of one field to another is similarly applicable to any pair of majors. For example, how or why is biology relevant to the study of politics? How or why can the study of art inform psychology? How or why is sociology invaluable to sports medicine? And again, in each case, course content should be applied as part of the rationale: The basics are still relevant.

One of the best exam questions I've ever heard of is from a physiology course. For their final exam, students are asked to argue for or against the feasibility of flying dragons, using their learning from the semester to justify their stance. This approach takes the phrase *contexts of uncertainty* to entirely new levels. Imagine the possibilities. Students in a political science course might be asked to imagine they are creating a new country from scratch. What branches or institutions of government would they choose and why? (Extra points for countries that do not replicate the American system.) Students in a course on psychology or neuroscience: Are smartphones and the way we use them going to change the biology of the brain and how it works? Base your arguments on biology and cognition.

These are more than your standard open-ended questions. In all three cases, students are asked to predict, create, and imagine, similar to the ways they'll be asked to think beyond the classroom once they've graduated. In all three cases, what matters is less the answer itself (although, of course, there's a range from *more right* to *very, very wrong*) than the mastery of the course material and the ability to apply that material in new or unusual situations.

This approach can be generalized even more. In most of my classes, I've taken to assigning a take-home final that asks students, "Tell me what you learned in this class that matters" (see Appendix D). This is essentially the same question as the previous ones but more wide open. Students need to determine the particular focus they'll take in terms of content, and they'll need to define what it means to matter. Does something matter because it received a lot of emphasis in the course? Does it matter because it's key to their major or their career goals? Does it matter because it connects to life outside the classroom? Does it matter intellectually or emotionally or spiritually? The responses I've received from a single class can be profoundly varied. In a recent class on artistic and literary responses to science and technology, student answers ranged from "What matters is less about 'what' than 'why'" to "Education should make us uncomfortable" to "I don't ever want to be a Prufrock" (T.S. Eliot's emotionally paralyzed narrator in the *The Love Song of J. Alfred Prufrock*).

This isn't to say that the question should lead to a free-for-all. On the contrary, students are told they must provide a clear and focused thesis that guides the entire essay, they must respond to the question analyzing at least three works we studied that semester, and they must apply the methodologies of the field, which in this particular case are close reading, attention to details in language, and analysis of possible meanings. Inevitably, I find this is one of the most rewarding parts of the course, which one can't often say about a final exam. To create a plausible response to this question, students must integrate and synthesize, drawing from a variety of works to find some common strand. And, of course, they are swimming in ambiguity. There is no right answer; they must create an answer and they must make meaning for themselves.

This question also gives me a clear sense of what's working in the course and what is not. As someone who's interested in continually improving his courses (I'm guessing we all are) it's helpful to know what connections are being made and what feels like random, meaningless information from the students' perspective. In my mind, everything I include matters in some way or another, but often this exam question teaches me that some connection isn't being made by some of the students, that some content feels like a dead end to them. That can be useful information for me as I revise the course for the next semester.

I can see this kind of question also being of use to professors in other disciplines. As students leave Organic Chemistry I for Organic Chemistry II, what connections are they making? Which ones are they missing? What matters to them? Is it the same that will matter next semester? If not, what can we do to revise Organic Chemistry I to foreground the contents and connections differently? In situations like this, the final exam for the course becomes not just an assessment of student learning but of the course itself, with the end goal of improvement (I discuss this more in chapter 7).

One final note, just in case readers are feeling overwhelmed by all these options or by the sense that course revisions of this sort will be a lot of work. They can be. But the rewards often outweigh the costs. With this take-home question, I get interesting insights into the minds of my students (sometimes *very* interesting); I get feedback on what's working and what's not in the course; I get high-end thinking from my students. What's more, because this question is a take-home portion of the exam, I can grade it while the students are writing the in-class part of the test. It really is a win-win-win situation.

Meanwhile, for those instructors who are feeling even more adventurous, I offer you an even more extreme exam option, advocated by many (Barkley, Cross, & Major, 2005), but perhaps articulated best by Bahls (2012). About a week and a half before the final exam, Bahls gives an assignment that asks students to write questions for the test, questions which may actually be included on the exam. Bahls lays out very clear criteria. For example, a sample question for a first-semester calculus course asks students to design a practical problem using kinetics: "Your problem should have at least two (related) parts and meaningfully involve each of *position, velocity,* and *acceleration*" (pp. 103–104). Multiple-choice or short-answer questions are not allowed. In addition, Bahls includes a peer review session to improve the quality of the questions, saying,

In asking students to take part in the construction of course material, we encourage them to become active authors of disciplinary knowledge. They deconstruct the ideas of the discipline, analyze them, question them critically, and reconstruct them. Crafting questions of appropriate difficulty and focus requires deep reflection on the concepts on which the questions are based. (p. 102)

In short, students are no longer passive recipients of knowledge in the course. They must go inside the material, get to know it not just as students but as teachers. They must own it.

---

### Designing Your Course: Step 10

1. Go back to your course topic and goals.
2. Brainstorm a list of radical exam questions you might ask your students. Think about bringing *integration, synthesis,* and *meaning making* into play, particularly in contexts where there is no absolute, right answer.
3. Set these questions aside for a few days, then come back and review them. Which ones stand up over time? Which ones might be revised to make them stronger?
4. Create a second list of these strong or revised questions.

---

## Multiple-Choice Exams

Years ago, I gave a workshop on my campus that included a sample multiple-choice quiz from one of my classes. Five minutes into my talk, a chemistry professor raised his hand and said, "I've never read the book, but I bet I can get all of these questions right." Then he did. Unfortunately, I'd forecast the right answers in a variety of subtle ways, including the length of the answer options, which choices had a parallel grammatical structure with the stem of the question, and so on. Students know these tricks, and they pay attention to them, so sometimes it's easy for someone who hasn't really done much work in the course to do well on the exam. Clearly, I was an amateur.

But some of the professionals in the game of multiple-choice exams also make costly mistakes. I've heard horror stories from students about one-hour exams that include 75 multiple-choice questions. Huh. I understand that it's important to teach our students to think on the fly, but . . . really? Because that allows 48 seconds per question. Then I've met professors who admit that a lot of the questions on their final exams are less about the content and more about students' ability to read carefully; put another way, the options the instructors provide in response to a particular stem are subtly written, with a word here or a word there making all the difference between right and wrong.

To some degree I understand this approach; I recognize the importance of careful reading, particularly in an age where all of us are bombarded constantly with language and ideas in various forms. But at the same time, unless we're spending as much time in our classes teaching careful reading as we are teaching content, then surely there's something inappropriate about this skill being the means of determining a student's grade.

I recognize that in situations when class size or the instructor's load prohibits written exams, multiple choice is the best option. But this raises the question of whether it is possible to create multiple-choice quizzes or exams that help develop authority in students. For me, there are two ways of thinking about this. The first has to do with the nature of the multiple-choice questions we ask; the second has to do with resources and efficiency in terms of how we use our time.

## Prompting Critical Thinking Through Multiple-Choice Questions: Exploring Some Options

Because I'm not an expert on multiple-choice testing—it's just not an approach that fits my field or my institution—I'm not going to write about question stems and distractors and so on. Plenty of experts know that material much better than I do, and I happily defer to their expertise. What I would like to do is propose a couple of small techniques that may help take our students beyond memorization even in the context of multiple-choice exams. I should note that I'm not arguing that all the questions on an exam should be of this nature. As I mentioned at the start of this chapter, I firmly believe there's nothing wrong with having questions that test basic factual and conceptual information. That's fair game. My argument, rather, is that if content testing is all we do, we're missing an opportunity to expose our students the kinds of complex situations that exist in many settings beyond the academy.

The first technique I'm suggesting is likely already familiar to many professors. Rather than providing students with one right answer and four incorrect distracters (which is a funny thing to include in any learning environment, if you think about it), we provide students with multiple correct answers and then have students justify the answer they choose.

This justification can occur in a number of different forms. One instructor I met spoke of starting class with a quiz that has several multiple-choice questions with single true answers (to test content knowledge) then ends with a question that has multiple correct possibilities. Once the quiz is completed, she takes an informal poll (possible even in large lectures) of who chose which answer for that last question. Then in a class discussion, students provide rationales for their various choices. Based on that, the instructor was then able to come away with a good sense of what students had or hadn't learned and was able to revise her lecture to fill in any gaps.

Of course, on a larger exam, this sort of conversation is generally not feasible. One alternative would be to place questions with multiple reasonable solutions toward the end of an exam, followed by a short-answer question such as, *In a paragraph or two, briefly justify the choice you made in the previous question. Refer to our readings, discussions, and lectures over the course of the semester.* Providing this option allows us to get a sense of how students are thinking, particularly in a more ambiguous situation, and in a way that doesn't require too much time on the part of the instructor (more on this later). In situations like these, the focus shifts from *What?* to *Why?* This is important, because the *Why?* helps us teach our students the kind of deliberate thinking that will be crucial when they step into the world and are bombarded by loud voices, obnoxious websites, and screaming memes, and must nonetheless make thoughtful decisions.

### Variation 1: Ambiguity Followed by Certainty

A variation of this approach is a series of cascading multiple-choice questions in which a student explains his or her thinking on an initial ambiguous question through follow-up responses such as the following:

22. Based on our readings in and discussion of *Do Androids Dream of Electric Sheep*, which is the *most likely* response Philip K. Dick would have to our contemporary smartphones?
    a. He would argue that they help us avoid silence.
    b. He would argue they can help us keep in touch with people we love.
    c. He would argue they let us see cat pictures, which is a good thing.
    d. He would argue that even electric things have lives, as pitiful as they may be.
    e. He would argue that they allow us easy access to beautiful art and music.
23. Which of the following responses best explains the choice you made in Question 22?
    a. Dick's emphasis on human superiority over androids
    b. Dick's emphasis on empathy as a valuable trait
    c. Dick's emphasis on the value of electronics to alter our moods
    d. Dick's emphasis on art as a defining component of being human
    e. Dick's emphasis on the complexity of what it means to be human

It's important to mention that this first question asks students to extrapolate their thinking beyond the novel in question. Dick's text was written in 1968 and doesn't say anything about smartphones. Therefore, the question puts students in that context of uncertainty that we're after. Additionally, in my reading of this novel and the discussions we've had the dozen or so times I've taught it, all the answers for that first question are arguably correct. That isn't to say that Dick would weight each response equally or even positively. I think, for example, that he would argue that avoiding silence is a bad thing but that having easy access to beautiful art and music is a good thing and that passages from the novel would bear this out. But all responses are certainly in the realm of an accurate reading of the novel.

The second question is a bit less ambiguous. Three of the answers (a, c, and d) are incorrect (again, based on years of teaching and discussing this novel, so no e-mails please). Option e is a reasonable answer, but only because it's a really vague statement. In the end, then, b is generally the best answer because by the end of the novel, Rick Deckard, the main protagonist of the book, feels empathy for androids and even for a small electronic toad. Meanwhile, J.R. Isidore, another major figure in the book, feels empathy for these entities all along.

Between these two questions, then, what we have is a moment of ambiguity followed by a moment of certainty. The first question familiarizes our students with uncertainty, preparing them for those moments, like the doctor in the examination room or the scientist in the laboratory, where there's no clear and easy path. Memorizing the facts helps, but finally, the students have to make a choice. The second question allows us to test basic knowledge. Have they done the reading? Do they remember the facts? Further, this second question helps us clarify how content relates to authority. Choosing an answer in the first question isn't just about opinion; it draws from something. There's a logic here.

Certainly, this approach is messy in some ways. Instructors testing this way have to decide how to grade that first question. Would all options receive full credit? Would only d (which I would argue is the best, most textually supported answer) receive credit? Would d receive full credit, and the others half credit? After all, all are true, but d is the best, and those who choose the best should get more points, right? In the end, these questions may seem consequential, but I'm not entirely sure that they are. We routinely give our students points for extra credit for questions that accomplish much less in terms of student thinking than the approach I'm advocating here. Does an extra point or half point really matter that much when it allows us to better position our students to deal with life in a complex world?

## Variation 2: Ambiguity Followed by Ambiguity

Consider the following option:

22. Based on our readings in and discussion of *Do Androids Dream of Electric Sheep*, which is the *most likely* response Philip K. Dick would have to our contemporary smartphones?
    a. He would argue that they help us avoid silence.
    b. He would argue they can help us keep in touch with people we love.
    c. He would argue they let us see cat pictures, which is a good thing.
    d. He would argue that even electric things have lives, as pitiful as they may be.
    e. He would argue that they allow us easy access to beautiful art and music.
23. Which if these responses best explains the choice you made in Question 22?
    a. Deckard's relationship with Rachel
    b. Dick's emphasis on empathy as a valuable trait
    c. Dick's use of artificial animals
    d. Dick's inclusion of Luba Luft and all that she represents
    e. Dick's unwillingness to draw clear lines between "humans" and "androids"

The first question here is exactly the same as the previous one. All are correct answers, but d is still arguably the best. The second question, though, has become much more ambiguous. All the answers have some degree of validity. Some of them relate directly to choices students might make in the first question: for instance, d for Question 23 is a perfect justification for choosing e in Question 22. Similarly, choosing c in the second question could justify choosing c in the first question.

One argument for this approach is that it continues to push students toward more complex ways of thinking. This isn't just about what's true anymore, it's about logic and connections and getting them to work in moments of ambiguity. Here again, we have multiple options for grading not just Question 22, but Question 23: All answers could get full credit, or the best answer (I'd argue d for 22, and b for 23) could get full credit and the rest get half. Students who are able to link correct answers from the second question to the first question get full credit on both, whereas students who don't would get half credit. Obviously, in the latter cases using any sort of test grading software becomes more complicated, but it's also possible that the data from a particular testing format would reveal some interesting information about how students are thinking, the kinds of logic they're using, or the answers or techniques they fall back on when faced with ambiguity.

### Variation 3: Ambiguity Followed by a Focused Justification

The following is another possibility:

22. Dased on our readings in and discussion of *Do Androids Dream of Electric Sheep*, which is the *most likely* response Philip K. Dick would have to our contemporary smartphones?
    a. He would argue that they help us avoid silence.
    b. He would argue they can help us keep in touch with people we love.
    c. He would argue they let us see cat pictures, which is a good thing.
    d. He would argue that even electric things have lives, as pitiful as they may be.
    e. He would argue that they allow us easy access to beautiful art and music.

23. Although there is no guarantee that option b is the correct answer in Question 22, what evidence from the text *might* best justify this option?
    a. Deckard's relationship with Iran at the end of the novel
    b. Dick's emphasis on empathy as a valuable trait
    c. Deckard's feelings toward the mood organs
    d. Deckard's feelings for Rachel
    e. Isidore's relationship with Pris

The purpose here is for students to think less about what is actually true or not than about What ifs? and contingencies. For example, we could rephrase the questions in the following ways:

- If b is true, what would justify that?
- Let us say that d is not true. Of the following options, some of which may not be textually accurate, which would best justify an inaccurate d?
- If d is a better option than b, what in the text would justify that, were it true?

The ways of framing a sequence of questions like this are endless. Indeed, one could even write a follow-up question for each of the options in the original question.

### Variation 4: Ambiguity Followed by an Explanation

A final variation derives from the work of Phyllis Blumberg (2009), who notes that it's not unusual for instructors writing exams to accidently create two options that are feasibly correct. Blumberg proposes allowing students to justify their "wrong" answers by citing references and explaining their own logic during the period between the return of the marked exams and the instructor's discussion of the correct answers. This is an excellent approach; perhaps we might even write this methodology into the exam itself, such as in the following:

22. Based on our readings in and discussion of *Do Androids Dream of Electric Sheep*, which is the *most likely* response Philip K. Dick would have to our contemporary smartphones?
    a. He would argue that they help us avoid silence.
    b. He would argue they can help us keep in touch with people we love.
    c. He would argue they let us see cat pictures, which is a good thing.
    d. He would argue that even electric things have lives, as pitiful as they may be.
    e. He would argue that they allow us easy access to beautiful art and music.
23. Which of the following responses best explains the choice you made in Question 22?
    a. Dick's emphasis on human superiority over androids
    b. Dick's emphasis on empathy as a valuable trait
    c. Dick's emphasis on the value of electronics to alter our moods
    d. Dick's emphasis on art as a defining component of being human
    e. Other (Please write your explanation in the following space)

The important component here is e in Question 23. In this context, "Other" is essentially a variation of the short-answer question suggested earlier in this chapter: In a paragraph or two, justify the choice you made in the previous question. This provides something of a win-win for students and instructor. Students have the option of providing an answer they feel is better than the options they are presented with, which allows them to explain their thinking. The instructor wins because instead of having 150 short answers that need to be graded, he or she may be faced with only 15, 30, or even 50, which is still better.

In the end, I find myself most comfortable with the option of a multiple-choice question followed by a short-answer question that allows room for articulation of thought. In my mind, this approach allows us to ask more complicated and integrative questions that move students in the direction of making new meanings and understandings. I recognize that I'm not in a situation where I have to grade 200 to 600 exams several times a semester. Still, I think it's crucial for us to continue to explore ways to ask multiple-choice questions that go beyond fact regeneration, that push students to not only memorize content but apply that content.

Two final points: First, as I mentioned earlier, any time we use nontraditional exam methods, we have an obligation to prepare our students in ways that are less high stake. This could be as simple as giving students quizzes or practice exams that model the strange beasts I've constructed in this chapter. Whatever method we use, the key is that students actually have a chance to *practice* answering the kinds of questions they'll encounter on the bigger exams. Simply lecturing will not be enough to shift students from test-taking methods they've become accustomed to for more than a decade to something completely different.

Second, questions structured along these lines require more time for students to complete. We're not asking for recall in these situations, we're asking for complex thought. We'll have to adjust our expectations in terms of the number of questions we ask, which leads us nicely into the next section. But first, let's look at Step 11, a brief exercise for those instructors who regularly use and would like or need to continue using multiple-choice exams.

---

### Designing Your Course: Step 11

1. Dig out one of your old multiple-choice exams and read through it, scoring each question on two scales:
   - Put a star next to every question that contains content that is absolutely essential for your field.
   - Give every question a critical thinking score of 1 (pure memorization), 5 (some critical thought necessary), or 10 (relies purely on critical thinking).
2. Keep all questions that have stars or score a 10; set aside the rest of the questions.
3. Working from the list of questions you've kept, experiment with the varieties of linked questions presented in this chapter. Be sure to
   - explore more than one option and
   - include at least a few more open-ended options that allow students to explain their thinking.
4. Once you've developed a good list of questions,
   - fine-tune them to make sure you're covering various aspects of the unit or course with enough breadth to ensure that students won't feel ripped off for studying everything;
   - make sure you're leaving enough time in the exam for students to think. The resulting exam may look uncomfortably short at first glance, but that's okay. This is about quality, not quantity; and
   - just because pure memorization can be good for our students, go back to the questions you set aside and reinstate 5 to 10 of them.

## How We Use Our Time: Rethinking Efficiency

One of the arguments I hear for giving multiple-choice exams is that they can be graded quickly and easily, that they are more efficient for the instructor. Although I'm wary of any definition of *efficiency* that focuses more on the instructor than on student learning, I'm nonetheless sympathetic to this argument. Many professors teach huge classes. Giving exams that include a long answer, or even short answers, simply seems impossible. Nonetheless, I'd like to poke and prod around the edges of this discussion of what is and isn't efficient when it comes to grading multiple-choice exams.

A friend who teaches economics at a large university is responsible for 3 classes, each with 190 students. Despite the size of these courses, all her exams include 2 or 3 short-answer questions at the end. She's able to assign these kinds of questions because, like many who teach large classes, she has several graduate teaching assistants (TAs) working with her to help grade the students' answers. Obviously, training those assistants to mark these questions consistently so that all students in all classes will be graded fairly takes some time. Chances are, training those graduate students to grade more authoritative questions fairly and consistently would take even more time.

But consider: If the final questions on an exam are purely content based, then norming discussions between the instructor and his or her research assistants must occur for every question on every exam. To ensure consistency, each question must be discussed by the entire group. In other words, if there are 3 short-answer questions on 4 exams, that means that there must be 12 discussions between the instructor and his or her TAs.

In contrast, more authoritative questions will likely require more conversation up front. The instructor will need to introduce the TAs to the concept of wicked problems and wicked answers, and there will need to be a discussion of how to mark the wide range of answers students might give for these questions. This conversation will not, however, need to occur 12 times, or even 8 times. It will take place once, maybe twice, just to check in and make sure the grading is consistent, but after that, the TAs need only check in with the instructor when they have a question about a particular student response. In the end then, the process of preparing graduate assistants, or even a group of instructors giving the same exam, may take slightly less time when the exam includes open-ended questions that push students toward integration and synthesis rather than open-ended questions that are strictly content oriented. We need to ask ourselves, then, which is really more efficient: 8 to 12 conversations about 8 to 12 exam questions that test low-end cognitive skills, or 2 to 3 conversations about 8 to 12 exam questions that test high-end thinking?

Perhaps I'm being idealistic. But even were the required time for the authoritative questions the same or slightly more, the decision to include them achieves two benefits we wouldn't otherwise see. First, our students would leave the exam having edged ever closer to their authoritative selves, aware that education means more than just memorizing facts. Given that most of these larger classes occur during the early stages of undergraduate education, this more expansive understanding of education is a good thing as it means that the further students get in our programs, the more self-reliant they are.

A second benefit is that our graduate assistants will leave the course with a sense of alternative possibilities. Most of our graduate students are the ones who performed well in the traditional paper-grinding and test-taking system. Education as it has been for the past 100 years has served them well. Unfortunately, if they become professors themselves, they'll be facing more and more students who are not like they were, students who increasingly come from underserved backgrounds, are first generation, were raised on a diet of high-stakes testing and teaching to the exam, and whose understanding of what it means to learn ends the second they hand in that final test.

In other words, by including our graduate students in conversations on wicked testing, we're better preparing them for the classrooms and the students they will be encountering. Further, we're providing them with some of the tools they'll need to help the students in those settings succeed beyond the classroom.

I want to add an additional thought on the topic of efficiency. I mentioned earlier the 1-hour exam that included 75 multiple-choice questions. Although I don't think that particular exam is a good idea, I do feel as though I understand the impulse behind it. We all care about our fields. We all recognize that in some way, shape, or form, everything in our field matters. So when we teach a chapter from a textbook or give a lecture, and we want to make sure the students know it, we test everything, or at least as much as we can.

What this way of thinking misses, though, is that it's not necessarily what happens in the exam that's important but what happens before the exam. In other words, just because we want students to know everything in a course doesn't mean that we have to test them on everything, just that they have to study everything.

I'm suggesting, in other words, is that there's no real value to giving exams that have 100, 75, or even 50 questions. At that point, even in a 3-hour test period, pure endurance is being tested more than deep knowledge. Exams like this are more of a stress test than an assessment of how much a student knows.

What's more, writing a test with even 50 questions takes a long time. Even once you've written an exam for a particular semester, you still have to rearrange the questions the next semester on the off chance that stray copies of previous tests are out there. If you teach multiple sections of the same course, it takes even more time desynchronizing the question order so that students in the 8:30 a.m. section can't aid students taking the test at 4:00 p.m. In the end, although long multiple-choice exams may seem time efficient, I'm not entirely convinced that they are, particularly not when placed against the ability of our students to go out into the world as something more than cubicle-bots.

What would happen then if instead of asking students 50 multiple-choice questions, we asked them 25? We would have to write fewer questions, but we could also write better questions that relied less on tricky wording and more on deep thinking on the part of our students. We would have to write our questions carefully, but we'd also have more time to do it. Meanwhile, students would still know they'd have to study all the material. They wouldn't know what would or would not be on the exam. Indeed, if anything, by the second or third exam they'd learn that it made some sense for them to prioritize their study habits. In other words, rather than just memorizing mindlessly, they'd begin to evaluate material, placing weight and value based on what they encountered in earlier exams. The only key here is that we need to offer enough questions covering enough variety of material to allow students to feel as though the mathematical probability of success justified extensive studying. If you have too few questions or questions that are too narrowly focused ("She gave us 15 questions on chapter 5, but nothing from chapters 1 to 4!"), students rightly feel that the game is fixed against them.

In addition to allowing us to write higher quality multiple-choice questions, such an approach also frees up more time for short-answer questions of the kind described in the first half of this chapter, questions that push students into the unknown, really requiring them to think. In the end, it would be nice if our exams could actually push students beyond what's been covered in class, asking them to take their thinking and learning a step further.

# 6

# DAY-TO-DAY
# TEACHING METHODS

A t Carroll Community College in Westminster, Maryland, the first thing meteorology professor Bill Kelvey does on the first day of class is hand students weather maps, put them in groups, and say, "Look at these maps, and tell me what's going to happen next with the weather." Then he lets them go at it (B. Kelvey, personal communication, June 1, 2015).

Physics professor Thomas Knorr used to begin his introductory physics lab (which included first-semester college students) by handing each of them a long piece of wood. Then he told them to design a unit of measure for their stick; it could be any unit, but they could not use a traditional method such as inches or centimeters. This method had to be devised entirely on their own, and they had to name it. Students were then required to use that unit of measure marked out on that piece of wood for the rest of the semester (S. Vargas, personal communication, June 15, 2016).

Both of these are first-day pedagogies, happening almost before the syllabus has been handed out. Both of them place students in challenging situations that they haven't been in before. Why do this on the very first day of class?

I hope by now the reasons are fairly obvious. First, these teaching practices begin the semester by giving students the sorts of problems they'll have to address in their field. A meteorologist needs to learn to read a weather map. A physicist needs to determine a method for measuring results with almost every new experiment. These pedagogies set the tone for the course, the major, and careers by saying to students, "This is what we do."

Second, both techniques push students to assume authority by insisting that they already have the mental capacity to figure out these problems. You can read a map. You can make educated guesses on what the lines, arrows, and numbers mean. You do not need to have your hand held as you tackle these problems. You may not get it completely right, but that's not what we're after. Even a 5% success rate is a start.

Third, as my colleague Chris Buchholz points out, the further students move into their courses, the more they read, the more they take notes in discussions and lectures, the more they practice, the more they will begin to master the material and see their own improvement over that first day. As a result, they begin to develop a growth mind-set that recognizes the relationship between simple things like doing the reading and succeeding in the course (C. Buchholz, personal communication, July 5, 2016). For many students, who assume you're either smart or not, this notion of cause and effect will be something of a revelation; their own progress becomes the motivation for further progress.

These kinds of first-day challenges thus establish a baseline that allows students to see the connection between a wicked ability to solve problems and mastery of course content. Recall the following equation presented in chapter 1:

CONTENT KNOWLEDGE + SKILL KNOWLEDGE
= A SENSE OF AUTHORITY

Because our goal here is to develop a sense of authority in all our students, not just those who have traditionally succeeded in college, a pedagogical approach that emphasizes development seems like a wise step.

The measurement challenge, and to some degree, the meteorology experiment, also make it clear that there isn't necessarily one perfect answer, that there might be multiple ways to approach a problem. Too often our first-year college students come to us with the high school mentality that there's always 1 and only 1 correct answer. For these students, being educated means simply memorizing and repeating that answer. As though every doctor facing every patient in the examination room immediately knows the "correct" diagnosis for each peculiar pattern of symptoms. As though every teacher walking into every classroom immediately knows exactly the perfect pedagogy to ensure learning for every individual student. As though every financial planner knows exactly what the market is going to do in the next 15 years, and can give her clients perfect, fail-safe advice every time. Life doesn't work that way.

Obviously first-day pedagogies like this are a great way to set the tone for your class and for a student's college career: "Life is full of uncertainties. But you can handle it. And we're in this together." I should also point out that neither of these assignments are graded very heavily. Indeed, the meteorology example isn't graded at all. Students work in groups, the class then discusses the results, and the professor uses these results to make some points about what students are already doing right, thus beginning to build their knowledge about how the science of this field actually represents and interprets data. The measuring stick assignment is graded but only very minimally. But of course, students are then required to use their measuring devices for the rest of the semester, sending an important message: What we're doing here matters and has consequences.

Implicit within all of this is the idea that if we're going to assign student authoritative projects like those described in chapter 4 or give them authoritative exam questions like those in chapter 5, we need to recognize that for most of our students, having come through an educational system built around just-the-facts testing, the kinds of tasks and tests described in this book are not just challenging and complex, but downright foreign. Additionally, we need to understand that it's unconscionable to require students to engage in authoritative tasks at high-stakes moments such as final projects or major exams without first giving them opportunities to practice these skills. Keeping these things in mind, we need to construct syllabi that allow students to practice the kinds of critical thinking we value throughout a course in

- increasingly complex ways; and
- in ungraded, minimally graded, or proportionally graded contexts.

The first criterion is fairly self-explanatory. As the semester goes along, the kinds of tasks we give students should move from relatively simple to relatively complex to very complex. Thus, the meteorology maps Kelvey gives his students on the first day will likely have minimal markings and fairly simple weather patterns. The maps he has them work with just before the final exam will have more data that are more complex with more potential outcomes. In between, students will practice the skills of map reading and weather prediction repeatedly. This repetition is key, because on a biological level, repetition strengthens neuronal networks, which leads to quicker, more accurate recall. One need only think of how frustrating it is to perform a complex task once a year—say, doing our taxes, or working the software for an annual self-evaluation—to understand how one-off performances don't lead to mastery.

The second criterion requires some explanation. The fundamental point is that the stakes during practice must be low. A large portion of learning has to do with messing up, stumbling, getting it wrong, reconsidering options, and trying again. The higher the stakes, the more this sort of necessary risk taking and experimentation becomes difficult for all but the most adventurous students. We need to construct at least some situations where completely fouling things up in a thoughtful way has little or no consequence for students. I like to think there are three ways to do this: in *ungraded, minimally graded,* or *proportionally graded* contexts.

*Ungraded* contexts means exactly what it says. Whatever task the student is performing does not receive a grade, no matter how many times the task is repeated. Even if the repeated task gets harder and harder, the results remain completely ungraded.

I should point out that like a lot of professors, I'm wary of giving too many assignments that have absolutely no consequence. I believe that weight toward the final grade is a rhetorical means of getting my students to pay attention. Consequently, I also consider as ungraded any series of smaller assignments in which the individual task or exercise receives a simple plus (for completion) or minus (for noncompletion). I explain this with an example later in this chapter. Suffice to say for the moment that I consider this ungraded work because in giving students a plus or a minus I'm not distinguishing between extremely high-quality work and stumbling, fumbling, still struggling to get it kind of work. Messing up and trying again is still legitimate for this type of assignment.

The second designation, *minimally graded* work, refers to the final weight any given assignment has toward the final grade in the course. I consider an assignment minimally weighted if it counts for 10% or less of the final grade.

The final method, *proportionally graded*, refers to a series of smaller assignments where the grade rises in increments as we progress through the semester. For instance, the first assignment might count for nothing at all, the second for 5%, the third for 10%, and so on. As the students get more practice, and the tasks become more complex, the grades rise proportionally.

## Three Case Studies

Allow me to give a few contextualized examples as a means of clarifying.

### Case Study 1: Geoscience

My colleague Chris Connors, a geoscience professor at Washington and Lee University, teaches students to analyze geological data sets to make mining or drilling recommendations in the following way:

- Early in the semester, students are given small data sets containing minimal *noise*—that is, data that are part of the soil sample but hold no real value or meaning. In these samples there are generally one or two fairly clear recommendations that the students can make.

- As the semester progresses, the soil data sets become gradually larger. Each contains a growing amount of noise with two or possibly three reasonable conclusions, all of which need to argued carefully.

- The final data sets in the course are very large. They include a great deal of noise; indeed, most of the set is noise, and they have multiple possible conclusions. These conclusions are not self-evident, and like the measuring device in Thomas Knorr's physics class, they must be constructed by each student.

- These assignments are *proportionally graded*. That is, the first ones count for perhaps 5% each, whereas the later sets could count for as much as 25% or 30%. (C. Connors, personal communication, May 5, 2013)

Quite clearly what's happening here is that students are moving from a place of near certainty to increasing ambiguity. By the final data sets, in fact, there really aren't any clear answers. Students must make sense of the data for themselves; they must make meaning. That there is room for error in the early assignments is crucial; if students mess up in those early sets, it's really not that big a deal. They have plenty of time left to recover before starting the later assignments that really count for a lot.

Crucial here is the fact that a series of assignments like this creates a continuous dialogue between student and instructor. Shortly after students attempt the task, they learn what they did right and where they went wrong. This is important on a biological level because a student who tackles a problem incorrectly essentially learns the wrong method, which is then imprinted on a neuronal level. Leave those neurons unchallenged, and they strengthen. If, on the other hand, a student tries something and very shortly thereafter gets feedback that it didn't work, then there's time and room to build on those incorrect networks (that prior knowledge) and develop a stronger, more accurate understanding. It's critical, then, for us to always provide opportunities for feedback in order to adjust students' learning.

Another thing I like about this geological example is how adaptable it is to different fields. Obviously, it works well in any social science course where learning to draw conclusions from data sets is a key goal. I would also argue, though, that it applies nicely to the humanities. After all, history students must also learn to sift through multiple documents—some primary, some secondary—to construct a meaningful and cogent narrative of what happened and why. And Connors's description of the movement from simple sets where meaning is relatively clear to large complex sets containing a lot of noise in many ways reminds me of moving literature students from short stories to Dickens's novels. At first, the data set is smaller, often with a single narrative arc. When reading *Bleak House*, on the other hand, the scholar is faced with multiple narratives and multiple plot arcs, some of which are more or less relevant to a particular critical question. Although I recognize this simplifies the complexities of meaning in narrative form, I find a great pleasure in recognizing that on a conceptual level what we're teaching our geologists and what we're teaching our literature students are not dissimilar. In both cases, an active mind must not just *find* a path but use the relevant data in a thoughtful, informed way to *create* a path.

## Case Study 2: Literature

The next series of assignments is drawn from a literature classroom, although again, I would argue that it's tranferable in a number of different fields. One of the goals in teaching literature at the university level is to move students from being passive recipients of a predetermined theme delivered by the instructor to active readers who are capable of creating a plausible meaning through close reading. A goal I have for my classes is for students to be able to construct incisive questions about a literary text and answer them in a thesis-driven essay. Years ago, a graduate colleague, Amy Goodburn, now at the University of Nebraska–Lincoln, introduced me to a series of group mini essays (see Appendix E). Here's how they work:

- Four times a semester, students have group project days, designated on the syllabus. Students work in the same group all semester long. (I assign groups, but others may choose to let students pick their own.)
- Every student comes to class with a typewritten question regarding that day's reading. These must be typed to ensure that students don't do them at the last minute. These questions should be thoughtful.
- After arriving in class, all students take a quiz. Those who pass the quiz get full credit for the essay that will be written later; students who do not, lose a full grade off the essay.
- Once the quiz is completed, students assemble into their groups and share questions. They have a discussion, then choose the question they think would lead to the best essay. (Obviously, I do some training with them ahead of time about writing effective questions.)
- Once they have a question, they create a Microsoft Word document. Two students are chosen by the group to be reporters. During class, the reporters will take notes as the group gathers quotations and discusses how to answer the question. Later, the reporters will draft the essay together in the same room at the same time.

- Once a draft of the essay is completed, the reporters are encouraged to share it with the group and get feedback. This is an important step, since everyone in the group receives the same grade for each essay, regardless of whether they were a reporter.
- Revisions of the drafted essay can be done by either the original reporters, or other members of the group.
- The final draft of the essay is turned in (usually about five days after the initial class), along with a group project log that details individual members' participation (see Appendix F).
- The essays should be roughly two typewritten single-spaced pages.
- Over the course of the semester, every student in every group must serve as a reporter at least once.
- Each of these mini essays is *minimally graded*, worth just 5% of the final grade for the course. Every group writes 4 essays, for a total of 20% of the overall grade (A. Goodburn, personal communication, April 12, 1993).

This series of projects is in preparation for a final individually written essay that requires each student to develop a question about a major reading from the semester and answer that question with a careful analysis of the text. This final essay is worth 25% of the overall grade.

There are several things I like about this assignment series. First, students are pushed off on their own to develop a question about the text. If truly effective reading begins with noting the contradictions and paradoxes in a text and seeing the things that don't make sense, then it seems imperative for us to turn this practice over to the students sooner rather than later.

The second benefit of this series of assignments is that it gives students repeated practice in the crucial skills of the course in a low-stakes way before dropping a big project in their laps. Too often we see syllabi in which students are passive for 12 weeks, sitting and listening and taking notes, then in the 13th week they're given a major assignment that asks them to think actively. Perhaps this approach works for our best students who walk into the class with plenty of experience and a strong sense of their capabilities, but for many of them, particularly our underserved and first-generation students, this all-or-nothing approach is a recipe for disaster.

It's worth pointing out that, unlike the geoscience assignment, this series doesn't have a natural increase in degree of difficulty built in. All four mini essays are essentially the same. In order to ensure that students don't get complacent with their learning, I make it a point in my classes to remind them that as they gain more practice with these sorts of assignments, my expectations increase. What might have received a B plus on the first paper will likely get a B minus or even a C plus on the third iteration. I think raising standards deliberately like this is useful because it pushes students to review the comments and feedback they received on the previous essays. If we're explicit in our application of increasing standards, students won't be inclined to just look at the grade while ignoring more detailed feedback. They must read the comments. (Or, if like many, their professors have moved to audio-visual feedback software like Jing, Camtasia, or Snagit, they must listen to the comments.)

As I mentioned earlier, I think this sort of mini essay approach is applicable to a number of different settings. I could see, for instance, an introductory sociology course where each assignment asks students to apply a theory from the text to a real-life situation beyond the classroom. Students in a psychology class might take a similar approach, even in an advanced-level course. This structure also works well for larger classes. I first used it as a graduate assistant when I was teaching courses with a cap of 44. Instead of assigning two individual essays and having to read almost 90 of those (very few of which showed much improvement from the first essay to the second) I assigned 4 group essays and 1 individual essay. Because my groups at that point consisted of 5 people, that meant that I received 9 essays 4 times a semester—a very manageable number—and 44 essays once a semester. Because students had received feedback on choosing questions and writing essays not just once but multiple times, I saw improvement in both the quality of the mini essays and in the number of students who turned in quality final essays. In short, although I graded essentially the same number of essays (in more manageable batches), I was getting better work, which was more enjoyable for both me and the students.

## Case Study 3: Physics

Years ago I was approached by a friend who was teaching a physics course in optics. She was unhappy with the quality of the lab reports she received. Although her students more or less knew the science, they seemed to have a very hard time articulating their knowledge in writing. She had attempted several nontraditional approaches, such as journal writing, and she still wasn't getting the kinds of writing she expected from emerging majors. The two of us sat down, brainstormed, and came up with the following:

- Typical for a class of this kind, students do 10 lab sessions over the course of the semester.
- After each lab, each student writes and turns in a full, traditional lab report.

- The science for each lab report is graded in terms of accuracy and effectiveness. Has the student performed the experiment correctly? Are the results as they should be? Is the math right?
- The written components of the lab report receive feedback—marginal comments, edits, suggestions, questions—but do not receive a grade.
- At midterm, students turn in a portfolio that contains
  ○ two lab reports in which the science portion is unchanged, but the writing has been revised based on instructor feedback, and
  ○ a brief rationale, one to two pages long, in which students explain why they chose to revise these two lab reports, the changes they made, why they made these changes, and anything they've consequently come to understand about physics, writing, or themselves.
- Students repeat this last step at the end of the semester, choosing two labs to revise from the second half of the term.
- Both of these portfolios receive a grade separate from the actual lab reports (Vargas and Hanstedt, 2014).

This is an example of an *ungraded assignment* because the writing portion that the instructor is focusing on doesn't receive a grade in the first iterations. Indeed, none of the writing in the 10 initial reports is graded. Consequently, students have room here to try, mess up, try again, mess up again, and eventually get better.

One could argue that this isn't really an authoritative assignment in that it doesn't have that component of pushing students off the deep end, forcing them to find solutions on their own. Okay, maybe so; but I don't know that argument matters. This is just good pedagogy. It gives students repeated practice at an important skill that will have an impact on their ability to succeed in their field after graduation. And it is worth noting that students who participated in this method often found that their science knowledge deepened. One student wrote the following:

> I believe that prior to the revision, I had no conception of the actual physical mechanism of the selective absorption of incident waves not polarized along the transmission axis. The rectification of my ignorance in this area of optics was a positive ramification of performing the revisions that is [*sic*] required by the portfolio submission. (Vargas & Hanstedt, 2014, p. 11)

Another student wrote,

> Looking back over my labs from the semester, it's clear that there is at least once where I didn't necessarily understand all the theory behind it, and it showed in the lab. For these two labs I really took the time to understand

what was going on and not only did my labs turn out better, I had a better grasp of the physics involved. . . . I took what was being taught in class and combined it with the work done in the lab and found that things made more sense than I thought they could. (Vargas & Hanstedt, 2014, p. 11)

This deepening of content knowledge is not really that surprising. For one thing, generally speaking, writing *is critical thinking*. Anson (2001) puts it this way: "As writers formulate thoughts into written propositions, their emerging texts loop back into their own thinking. Words written become words reconsidered, ideas put to new tests" (p. x). In other words, as we put words down on paper, we look at the ideas they represent and wonder not only is that really what we meant to say, but also, is that really true? Carefully assigned writing pushes us to test our ideas, thereby deepening our learning. Metacognitive writing of the sort assigned here, where students actually examine and think about their own learning, perhaps pushes critical thought even more effectively. As Maki (2010) states, "Self-reflection reinforces learning by engaging learners in focused thinking about their understanding *and* misunderstanding" (p. 48).

Of course, if an instructor wanted to make Vargas's assignment even more authoritative, he or she could pull back some of the feedback on the written portion. For example, instead of doing line edits on every page of every lab report, the instructor could provide comments on only the first two pages, then tell students, "Please be sure to apply the kinds of advice I've already given you to the rest of the essay." This method ensures that students will not simply follow instructor comments; instead, it pushes them to take some responsibility for the development of their essay. Additionally, as Bean (2011) notes, it keeps the instructor from getting buried with a load of editing work. Alternatively, an instructor could provide more line edits and comments earlier in the semester, and as the semester unfolds give more and more responsibility to the students.

In either case, or even as this assignment stands now, part of the reason all this works is because it requires students to act on the feedback they receive. Unlike the student who receives the paper, project, or exam at the end of class, glances at the grade, and dumps the product of all those hours of work in the trash on the way out the door, this series of assignments carries out Zull's (2002) cycle of deep-learning. Once students receive information regarding their performance, they're asked to think about it (in this case in written form in the reflective essay that is part of the portfolio) and then act on their ideas, experimenting, trying things, and taking steps to make their work better. Then they receive feedback on this second attempt, and the cycle continues. In other words, learning deepens, it does not just stop at the grade.

Finally, I chose to include this approach to lab report writing because it demonstrates a crucial point. When we're designing daily pedagogies to support student learning, it isn't necessarily an all-or-nothing gambit. Part of the reason this approach works for Vargas is because she separates the science from the writing. She's comfortable with her students' ability to handle the science, so this process only nails the part she's not happy with: the written communication. This makes sense. Given our busy schedules, there's no point wasting time or energy on student skills that are already in good shape.

I want to make one important note before I have you apply some of what we're discussing to your own courses. Very often when I've presented these ideas in a workshop, one or two faculty members will develop a series of assignments wherein additional tasks are layered into each new iteration. For instance, a professor attempting to teach students how to write effective lab reports may only require students to write the introduction to the report the first time, the introduction and the methods the second time, the introduction, the methods, and the results the third time, and so on.

I understand the logic behind this. If our desire is to have students practice skills repeatedly and at increasingly challenging levels, this would seem to fit the bill; they write the introduction several times, only each time is harder because there's an added task that they also must perform, such as writing the methods, then writing the methods and the results, and so on.

While I think there's some wisdom to this approach, I don't think it entirely gets at what we're after here: For instance, it may result in crucial and complex skills receiving less practice if they're layered in late; it may ignore necessary logical connections between one area and another (say, methodology and conclusions); it can be awkward to grade; it may work against what we know about how working memory and executive function in the brain use repetition to prioritize between simple and complex tasks. Finally, though, I wonder if it doesn't violate one of the maxims we discussed in chapter 2 during our discussion of goals: Always challenge students. By letting students wade in gradually—first the toe, then the foot, then the ankle, then the shin, and so on—we send the message that we don't trust them to do the work of scientists or of art history scholars or of economists: "You're not ready yet. We're going to take baby steps."

In my mind, this is a missed opportunity. Say what they will, but on some level when students come to college they want to be adults, they want to be challenged, and they want to feel like they are doing real work, not just fulfilling random expectations. Whenever possible, then, we should capitalize on that impulse from the very beginning. Have them do real meteorology on the first day, make their first lab be a real lab; tell them their first literary exegesis is to be of a complete poem, not just a part of a poem. This leaves room for real success and real failure and real consequences for not quite getting things right. This also allows students to see the big picture right away to have a sense of how all the parts fit together. The stakes are raised at the second (and third and fourth) iterations not by adding more pieces but by raising the degree of difficulty of the overall task, by moving it toward the kinds of complexity that scientists actually encounter in the lab and that literary scholars actually encounter when analyzing texts.

Having said that, there are no hard and fast algorithms when it comes to pedagogy; if you see a way to layer additional processes or content that you feel will serve your students, give it a try.

---

### Designing Your Course: Step 12

1. Choose one of the assignments or test questions you drafted in chapters 4 and 5.
2. Brainstorm for five minutes, thinking about any day-to-day tasks you already have in your class that allow students to practice the skills necessary to succeed for this assignment or exam.
3. How might you structure these pedagogies or tasks into your course in ways that allow
   ◦ repetition?
   ◦ increasing levels of difficulty?
4. Should these tasks be *minimally graded*, *proportionally graded*, or *ungraded*?
5. Jot down some notes on all of this.

---

## Additional Examples

What follows are 19 additional pedagogies I've encountered over the years that have the potential for developing authority in our students—and, frankly, are just darn good methods for teaching. I've included less annotation in this portion of the chapter, working from the assumptions that you know your field and your students better than I do and that as experienced professionals, we've developed the wicked capacity to adapt techniques and methodologies from one setting to another. When considering these ideas, then, take a moment to think about each and how it might be revised, reconsidered, or restructured for your institution, your students, your field, your courses, and most important, your goals. Always begin by asking, "I wonder if...?"

Further, keep in mind the purpose of these techniques: to shift the responsibility for learning from the instructor to the students. This is crucial because at first glance some of these look like fun practices designed solely to keep the students engaged and active. Although what follows are active methods that will engage students, their most important feature is that they place students in situations where they must own the course material and work with it in ways that are risky, problematic, or unsolvable. In the end, students must come to understand that this is how learning—and life—work.

## Generating Questions: Ungraded or Minimally Graded

When students arrive in class, they are asked to generate three questions related to the day's reading. Some of the questions can relate to pure content and understanding, but at least one of the questions should be something they believe would lead to an interesting discussion. (Note: This technique can be used even in large classes where discussion might never occur.)

Once the students have generated lists individually, they pair up or form groups of three, look at their lists, and generate a new list of three exemplar questions. Students must be able to explain why these questions are worth discussing. The only rule here is that they can't take all three questions from one person's list.

Although this task may appear to waste time in that it cuts into the minutes available to actually discuss questions, in reality, as students first generate and then select questions, they're already thinking about what matters, what doesn't, and about some of the answers and potential answers to these questions.

## Epigraph and Analysis: Minimally Graded

Students come to class with a one-page typewritten response to the day's reading. At the top of the page, they include a quotation from the reading. This quote can be something they love, hate, are confused about, or think is relevant to the class.

The rest of the page contains a careful analysis of their response to the quotations: What do they love about it? What do they hate about it? Why do they think it's relevant to the class? What word or words confuse them? How do they see this quotation as applying to their lives? To other readings? To other courses? To their long-term goals? To their learning?

I've seen this technique used in a number of different ways. Some instructors collect the responses and give them a check or minus. Others choose two every day (from different students) and use them to begin discussions.

Still others have students exchange the responses, find hot spots or smart ideas, and use those as the basis of the discussion that day.

Some instructors require a reading response like this every day, although others require it only once a week. I generally respond to these pieces in detail only when I have lots of time. On the other occasions, when I'm buried in work, I'll sometimes just put a check or minus at the top of the page, which I refer to as "white wine grading," a phrase that I'm fairly certain requires little explanation. In the end, this kind of writing is less about students showing me what they know and more about their exploring ideas and using writing as a means of exploring ideas. Practicing this skill isn't always something that needs a lot of instructor feedback. I count this activity between 10% and 15% of the overall grade because I do think this sort of thought process matters. If students don't turn in at least 70% of these requested responses, they receive an F in the course.

### Response Theses: Minimally Graded

Students arrive in class with three typewritten theses related to that day's reading. These are shared and discussed, either in small groups or with the class as a whole, as a means of developing thesis-writing skills and of catalyzing the discussion. I grade these with a check or minus.

### Case Studies: Minimally or Proportionally Graded

I covered a version of this method in chapter 3 as a means of organizing the overall course, but case studies can also be a useful day-to-day exercise. Periodically throughout the semester, present students with brief, puzzling cases and ask them to propose solutions based on the reading, lectures, and discussions. The nature of these cases should obviously be determined by the content of the course, but as much as possible they should be contextualized in terms of life beyond the academy. In other words, throwing a math problem on the board is not a case study; couching that math problem in statistical analyses of the weather, gun control, or poverty in developing nations, however, is a case study because at this point these issues become appropriately wicked. The case studies should become increasingly complex as the course progresses and students begin to gain control over the material.

### Send a Problem: Ungraded or Proportionally Graded

In a variation on case studies from Barkley (2010), various groups or pairs of students are each given different problems or case studies and asked to propose solutions based on the best thinking in the field as they've thus far learned it. Once students have completed this task, they pass their problem on to another group and then receive a new problem. Without looking at the previous group's solution, these new groups tackle the problem, making their own proposal. The material is passed on and the process repeated at least three times. Once the final group receives the problem, their task is to examine the various solutions and analyze and synthesize them, reporting to the class as a whole which solution (or hybrid solution) they think is best.

As Barkley (2010) points out, this technique involves problem-solving and evaluative skills. In today's digitized world, where we're encountering more and more solutions but fewer and fewer thoughtful ones, developing this skill is crucial.

### Two-Sided Debates: Ungraded

Students are separated into two or more teams and asked to develop arguments for *both* sides of a particularly complex or divisive question, drawing from readings, lectures, discussions, and research. They should be told that extra points will be given for their ability to not just cite data, but *explain* that data in a way that would make sense to someone not in this class. Additional points are given to the team that has the most members who take an active speaking role.

Once they've had time to generate material for both sides of the question, then and only then are sides appointed. The debate that follows should involve an initial statement of ideas, responses to each side, and closing arguments. If you wish, you may give teams time to discuss their ideas between segments.

The instructor should then lead an analysis and discussion of the debate. Which side did better? Why? If their team had been assigned the opposite side of the debate, what arguments might they have added to the discussion?

If you have a larger class, there's nothing wrong with creating four, six, or even eight teams and having them all go through the same process, collecting data for both sides, having a side assigned to their team, and so on. You might then have one group make the opening argument, another the response, and still another the closing argument. Regardless of how many groups there are, the key is that all groups consider both sides of a complex question, whether or not they actually make a presentation.

### Mock Trial: Ungraded (assuming it isn't developed into a more extensive assignment)

This is a variation on the preceding debate technique, although it can be turned into a more extensive assignment. Once course content has been

presented through lectures, readings, or discussions students are introduced to a case that is relevant to the content. For example, in Stoddart and
McKinley's (2006) section of their psychology course exploring sleep, they
use a real-life case in which a husband offered sleepwalking as his defense for
stabbing his wife in the middle of the night. Students are put in groups and
asked to prepare the defense and prosecution, then they are assigned to one
side or the other, and a trial proceeds.

## No Preread Paper (or Project) Conferences: Ungraded

We know from years of research that one of the best ways to improve both
the quality of the thinking and the quality of the writing in student papers
is to require students to do multiple drafts (Bean, 2011). Unfortunately,
sometimes managing the revision process can be burdensome for instructors
and debilitating for students. Consider, for example, the traditional method
for holding writing conferences: The student turns in a draft at least a day
before the scheduled conference, the instructor goes over that draft that evening, and the next morning the students sits in the instructor's office quietly
taking notes as the instructor tells them what they should do to make the
paper stronger. Certainly, some instructors ask questions or push students to
develop work-plans, but the implicit message is that the instructor wanted
the paper ahead of time because it's his or her responsibility to tell the student
what to do, not the student's responsibility to decide how to move forward.

This approach takes a lot of work. Even if a professor only has a dozen
students, it requires reading and commenting on a dozen drafts the evening
before the conferences, not to mention carving three or four hours out of a
busy day to actually meet with students. One alternative method is no pre-
read conferences. With this model, all students turn in papers on the same
day, at the same time, generally the first day of conferences. As the name
implies, the instructor does not read those papers ahead of time. Instead,
when the student comes into the office, the instructor asks him or her to take
out a notebook and pen. Then the instructor asks the student to make the
following three lists:

1. Name all the changes the student already knows he or she would like to
   make to the draft. These might include things the student forgot about,
   didn't have time for, that came up in class that morning, or that occurred
   to the student while walking to the instructor's office. These are for sure
   changes, changes the student definitely wants to make.
2. Name all the maybe changes. That is, the ideas the student has for possible revisions but is not quite sure about. Maybe these are things the

student tried earlier that didn't work, something he or she would like to do but is pretty sure is a bad idea, or just something nagging in the back of his or her head.

3. Questions the student has for the instructor concerning this paper.

While the student makes these lists, the instructor quickly reads through the paper, paying attention to general trends that stand out, particularly at the level of ideas, thesis, evidence, or paragraphing and organization. The instructor might also notice glaring patterns of grammatical errors but shouldn't get too distracted by these, as they may be corrected in subsequent revisions (Bean, 2011). Note that reading or skimming drafts may take a bit longer the first few times an instructor uses this method (and not uncommonly for the first few papers of a particular assignment), but eventually the instructor will get a sense of the types of issues students are encountering with a particular assignment, and this part of the process will move more quickly in later conferences.

Once the instructor and the student have finished their tasks, the instructor asks the student to go through the lists, explaining them one at a time. At this point, the instructor and the student should become involved in a dialogue, talking back and forth about each suggested change, particular ways of implementing good ideas, or questions surrounding any sketchy ideas. The student should be taking notes.

The key here is that unlike traditional conferences, the responsibility for the paper is clearly on the student whose ideas are driving the conversation; all the instructor is doing is responding to those ideas, offering advice, affirmation, or thoughtful skepticism when necessary.

## *Monday Morning Riddles: Ungraded*

This idea is from Dan Clark at Western Oregon University. The title is self-explanatory. The first thing every week, students are presented with a problem to be solved (D. Clark, personal communication, June 6, 2016). A physics professor intent on having his or her students eventually develop a method for calculating the number of blades of grass on the football field asks students to figure out a method as a group for calculating the number of desks in the building or the number of ceiling tiles in all the classrooms on the first floor. A literature professor intent on getting students to recognize how a single poem may offer multiple meanings presents a poem by Christina Rossetti, provides two contrasting analyses, and asks students to debate which is correct. A philosophy professor teaching logic offers his students a syllogism and asks if it's correct. A mathematics professor simply writes a complex problem on the board and asks students to collaboratively discuss how to solve it. As the semester progresses, the instructor might even choose to ask students to bring in problems, riddles, or puzzles they've encountered that are appropriate for the class.

Key here is that the riddle is solved collaboratively, involving both the instructor and the students. This kind of exercise can even occur in a large lecture course.

### Real-World Applications: Minimally Graded

This approach can be implemented using a number of formats: class discussions, journals, wikis, or blogs (Barkley, 2010). It can also apply both to course content or to skills that are taught in the course (Ambrose et al., 2010). Essentially, this technique asks students to make connections between the course content and the real world. What theories have they encountered in the course that help them understand the current political situation? What solutions have they encountered that they might propose in response to the immigration debate? How is Victorian literature relevant to twenty-first-century life? How effective is the mainstream media at reporting on science?

Two things are necessary to make this technique work. First, students must be absolutely required to clarify exactly what course content they're connecting to the outside world, be it a passage from a textbook, part of a lecture, or something they encountered in a lab session. This is to ensure that students are avoiding generalizations as they try to master content and apply it beyond the classroom.

Second, students should be required to do more than simply describe the connection. Yes, they should talk about what they see in the class and what they see outside class. But then what? Why does this matter? What is revealed about the course content, about the real world, about learning, about the student and how he or she views the world, about what may happen next? Description matters, but it allows the brain to stay relatively passive. Answering the "So what?" question pushes students toward higher levels of cognition, the kind that deepen learning and strengthen a sense of authority.

### Jigsaw: Ungraded, Minimally Graded, or Proportionally Graded

This method works well when a series of small pieces are necessary to solve a larger problem. Essentially, the term *jigsaw* refers to breaking up things and putting them back together, in this case, the day's content and the various groups of students. Here's how it works:

1. If I have assigned five poems to class that day (or five poets, or five calculations, paintings, or philosophers), I divide the class into five groups, assigning each group one piece of the puzzle, whether a poem, a poet, a calculation, or a painting.
2. Each group has to answer the same series of questions about the poem (poet, calculation, etc.). Every student in the group must take notes because they will then report the findings of the group they are presently in to a second group that will be formed shortly.
3. After these first groups have had adequate time to answer the questions, I break them apart and create new groups, each containing one member from each of the first groups. This is to ensures that all of the new groups can now hear the findings from each of the previous groups. In other words, if I had five groups of five, I'll now make five new groups of five, with every new group containing one member from each of the first groups; if I had three groups of five, I'll now make five groups of three, again, with every new group containing one member from each of the previous groups. The key here is that every student in the class is responsible for reporting the findings of his or her first group to his or her second group.
4. Each group member reports to the new group what the previous group discovered, that is, the answers to the questions provided by the instructor (number 2).
5. The new groups then use the aggregate data to solve a new and complex problem.

This final step of solving a new problem that depends on the information from the first set of groups is another crucial component to making this exercise work. This step gives meaning and significance to the reporting process. Every student must master the material from the first group, understanding it well enough to bring it to the second group. If they don't, the second group won't be able to accomplish the final task.

For example, on the first day of the class on Romanticism and Romantic philosophies, I give the first set of groups the following questions:

1. How does the writer view nature?
2. How does the writer view society?
3. What does the writer seem to see as the purpose of poetry?

The students will discuss these questions with the members of their first group. All of the students will be taking notes so that they can then report out to the second set of groups. Once the first set of groups have all finished answering the questions, the students will be placed in new groups tasked with using the information gathered earlier to complete the following assignment: "Using the information generated in the first groups looking at five different poems, what are Romanticism's goals? What's the agenda of the Romantic poets?"

This exercise works slightly differently in different courses as the instructor seeks to prepare students for different tasks. For instance, in chapter 4 I mention the following assignment when discussing a first-year seminar on public art.

> Create a proposal for a local public mural in the Dover area for possible grant or funding applications. Include and prepare a rationale for a description of the project, several means of creating community input and involvement, the long-term goals for community impact, and a budget.

To get the students ready for this complex final project, the instructor could construct a series of jigsaw exercises stretching over weeks that present students with case studies of various communities. Rather than all the first set of groups doing the same task, however, in this situation each group might be given a different piece of the puzzle. One group may be asked to examine the material and figure out a means of creating community input, another group may be asked to develop goals, and another may be asked to explore funding agencies. Then, once reassembled into a second set of groups, students may be asked to examine the ideas, materials, or data generated in the first groups and propose an initial description of a mural. As long as the students know they will be responsible for reporting from one group to the next, and as long as the second groups are provided with a complex task that makes use of the outcomes of the first groups, the jigsaw exercise can be structured in any number of productive ways.

## *Think Again: Ungraded*

On the face of it, this activity may appear a little cruel, but its purpose is pure. At the start of class, the instructor places a statement on the board. It should not be factual but rather should require some interpretation of the day's reading. Indeed, this technique works best when it related to something that most students will likely get *wrong*, at least initially.

The instructor should then ask students to respond to the statement on the board by writing true or false on a sheet of paper, alerting them that once they've written an answer, they will not be allowed to change it. The instructor should ask all the students who wrote true to gather on one side of the room. Those who wrote false are to cluster on the other.

The instructor then provides the correct answer without explaining it. The students on both sides of the room (working as a group, or at least in pairs) are then asked to use their notes, readings, class discussions, lectures, and so on to explain their reasoning behind the correct answer. The results generated by the two groups should then be compared (Barkley, 2010).

The purpose of this assignment is to move students beyond obvious or first-impression thinking and then to show them that they have and have had the capability to arrive at the correct answer all along. Indeed, more often than not the results between the correct group and the incorrect group are very similar. In short, this method teaches more deliberate thinking. It also teaches those who haven't done the reading that they're missing out on content that will be used in class.

## Generating Images: Ungraded or Minimally Graded

In *The Art of Changing the Brain*, cognitive neuroscientist James Zull (2002) notes that learning is deeply indebted to the senses and that our visual sense is arguably one of the most powerful of these: "If we can convert an idea into an image, we should do so. And wherever possible, we should require our students to show us their images" (p. 146). Zull goes on to say that although it's easy to think about how certain topics can easily be translated into images—he cites mathematics as one of the most "image-dependent subjects"—others such as music or philosophy may seem to be a less natural fit (Zull, 2002, p. 146).

His point, and mine, is that the more abstract the concept, the more necessary it is to have students create images that allow them to visualize these abstractions to aid their recall. For instance, one of the dominant schools in the field of composition and rhetoric is social epistemic theory, that is, the belief that our understanding of the world is mediated through language, that conceptions of what is true and good and possible are changing continually and that teaching writing is never an apolitical act (Berlin, 1988).

Needless to say, when many of the education majors at my institution first come across this theory, they're rattled. Reality is mediated? Truth is continually changing? "I just want to teach third graders how to write!" they say. Over the years I've learned that discussing this theory only helps so much. Pointing to the text and dissecting particular passages only helps so much. Watching me stand at the board, drawing complex diagrams and waving my arms only helps so much (and may lead to comments mocking my artistic failings). What students need to do is take a marker in hand and generate an image representing this theory. Some have drawn treadmills to represent the ever-changing nature of truth, beauty, and possibility, sketching in letters along the treads to represent the role language plays. Others have created images of a person climbing a ladder with flames at the bottom to represent the high stakes in writing, the power dynamics that are always there and always threatening to burn those who are often on the outside of traditional discourse.

This activity can be transferred to any number of fields. I have a colleague in biology who has students create a cartoon comprehensible to anybody, even those not in the course, depicting the transcription of DNA into RNA, and the translation of RNA into protein (Hanstedt, 2012). Although this image generation might not be directly related to any final assignment we give, it can still be an authoritative tool in that it requires students to understand the course material from the inside out, to very literally make it their own. And again, remembering Zull's (2002) earlier point, these images improve the chances of deep learning and greater recall.

## Concept Maps: Ungraded or Minimally Graded

Related to the preceding approach, and likely more familiar, are concept maps or knowledge maps. Essentially, these are images representing ideas, facts, and data with an emphasis on, as Blumberg (2009) puts it, "showing the *relationships* among the concepts, such as cause and effect, consequences, or a series of events" (p. 95). Flowcharts and tables are concept maps, but students should by no means feel limited to these forms. Nothing says that images couldn't just as easily replace boxes in a flowchart, or that "flow" might not somehow demonstrate the kinds of commonalities and disconnects illustrated with a Venn diagram.

In short, as with image generation, the goal here is for students to assume authority as they learn the logic or logics of a concept being taught in the course. As Blumberg (2009) noted, these knowledge maps can be generated individually or collaboratively or both, using one and then the other.

## Gallery Walks: Ungraded

Gallery walks build nicely on the previous pair of activities, essentially putting the images and concept maps generated by students on display for the entire class to see, allowing for dialogue and feedback that can lead to productive revision (B. Tewksbury, personal communication, May 19–22, 2008).

The logistics are simple. Once the images or concept maps (or for that matter, drafts of formal posters) have been generated, they are hung on the walls of the classroom. Students then peruse the gallery, considering the work of their peers and asking questions and offering feedback. This part can take place in a number of different ways; for example,

- Students are simply given yellow sticky notes and asked to create questions and ideas for at least 5 (or 3 or 10) different posters. (Note: It's a good idea when using this approach to coach the class on effective and constructive feedback.)

- Half the class strolls around looking at the images, maps, and posters; the other half stand by their posters explaining and answering questions. Then the two halves switch so that everyone gets a chance to see the work of the others, and they all get a chance to explain, defend, or expand on their ideas.
- The instructor goes around the room, drawing everyone's attention to each poster and leading impromptu discussions of their strengths and strategies to improve them.
- Any or all of these methods can be combined.

Gallery walks have several obvious benefits. First, they raise the stakes for the images and maps by creating a real audience. Any time we know that real people with real questions and real thoughts in their real heads are going to be examining our work, we become much more focused and thoughtful in our approach.

Second, if we use the option of having half the students standing by their posters for a question-and-answer defense of their images or charts, the stakes are even higher. As the students are pushed to explain their thinking orally, they gain further mastery over the material and likely improve their sense of authority, coming to understand that they can do this, that they are capable of discussing these complex subjects.

Third, by being asked to offer feedback to their peers, students are also developing a sense of authority. Let's face it, being a member of the audience can be an invigorating experience, especially if part of one's role is to offer a critique. We may not exactly be an expert on the topic at hand, but all of us are experts on being confused, not understanding, or being able to say to the presenter, "Right *there,* that idea, that thing you said, *that's* what confused me. What did you mean by that?" And very often, as audience members, we see logical flaws in the work of others that we wouldn't notice in our own efforts, which then allows us to turn back to our poster or map and revise and strengthen it.

## *Think-Aloud Pair Problem Solving: Ungraded*

This technique from Barkley and colleagues (2005) works well in classes that require a lot of problem-solving. The basic technique involves the instructor coming to class with a number of field-related problems that can be solved within a relatively short period of time. Although the problems themselves should be challenging, they should allow students to engage in some of the basics of problem solving such as identifying the problem, analyzing the knowledge and skills necessary for solving it, brainstorming possible solutions, and so on.

Students form pairs in class and are given a problem. One of the students is asked to talk through the problem-solving process, and the other is asked to listen carefully, understand the thinking as much as possible, and offer suggestions where issues or missteps seem to occur. Then, the students switch roles. The listener becomes the problem solver, and the problem solver becomes the listener.

Part of the appeal of this technique is in the following rationale provided by one of the case studies in Barkley and colleagues' (2005) work in which a set of problem-solving questions for a computer science course are discussed:

> Students needed to become competent in a complex problem-solving process of retrieving, manipulating, and analyzing sequences from a variety of databases. The instructor noticed that some of his students "caught on" and were able to go through the steps relatively easily. Others tended to make process mistakes that resulted in programming errors that were time consuming and frustrating to find later. Historically, these struggling students simply dropped the course at this point, so the instructor was searching for ways to reduce attrition and alleviate student anxiety. . . . the result was that students not only gained competence sooner than in the previous semester when they worked independently, but it also significantly improved student retention. (p. 261)

Too often, students and sometimes instructors approach authority as though it is something you either have or you don't. I don't agree. I believe we can teach these ways of thinking, that we can shift a students' attitudes and shape their sense of what they're capable of by putting them in situations that challenge them and also teach them how to succeed.

### *Generating Rubrics: Ungraded, but Stunningly Useful*

This is a method brought to my attention by Hannah Robbins, one of my colleagues in mathematics. Although this particular example is designed for oral presentations (she uses it in her mathematics courses and her general education courses), it's easy to see how it might be adapted for almost any kind of academic work we ask our students to turn in.

Rather than present students with an instructor-designed rubric that many of them may find confusing and some of them will never read, Robbins gives two presentations, one good and one containing all the mistakes she'd like her students to avoid.

Once she's done that, she has students brainstorm several lists on the board, asking them what was good about her presentations. what was not, and why? Then she leads them in a discussion that pares this list into a series of tips for giving a good presentation. She posts these tips on the class website and uses it as a rubric for grading their work (H. Robbins, personal communication, June 13, 2016).

## Generating Study Questions: Minimally Graded in a White Wine Kind of Way

Early in the semester, the instructor provides students with study questions for the first unit exam. As the semester progresses, the students begin to generate some of their own questions for successive exams with guidance from the instructor. As the semester ends, the students develop their own questions for the final exam, with little or no guidance from the instructor (Blumberg, 2009).

Essentially, this exercise shifts responsibility from the instructor to the student for creating the bridge between course intake—that is, all the content students learn from lectures, readings, discussions, and labs—and course output, that is, the exams and quizzes. As a result, this approach creates more active readers who, rather than reading passively, are constantly asking themselves, What matters here? as they flip through the chapters of their texts. Students are engaged, then, in evaluation from the far right-hand side of Krathwohl's (2002) taxonomy. But they're also engaged in projection and construction, asking, What kind of question might be on the test? How might this material be brought into play? So again, they're operating on a higher cognitive level. This technique might easily be used in combination with Bahl's (2012) method for student-generated exam questions, discussed in chapter 5.

---

### Designing Your Course: Step 13

1. Choose one of the assignments or test questions you drafted in chapters 4 and 5. (It may be the same as earlier in this chapter, or it may be different, it's entirely up to you.)
2. Choose two of the activities in this chapter and explore
   ○ how you might adapt them to your particular assignments; and
   ○ where you might place them in your syllabus so that that students may practice the necessary skills repeatedly and with increasing levels of difficulty.
3. Should these tasks be *minimally graded, proportionally graded,* or *ungraded?*
4. Think of one or two additional, completely new activities that do not appear in this chapter and that may also help your students learn the skills and contents necessary to complete your assignment.
5. Repeat as necessary for other assignments or exam questions.

# INTERMISSION

## Putting It All Together: Part Two

At this point, you're probably exhausted. Too much information, too many ideas. Take heart, this next step is crucial, but it is the last move you'll have to make. Simply put, it's now time to put things together.

As with the previous Intermission, I strongly recommend that you change your medium and use a form you're less familiar with. Indeed, probably the best way to complete this exercise is to create a poster using poster board or butcher paper.

Step 1: Reexamine your goals in light of the thinking you've been doing in the previous three chapters.

- Are there any obvious and necessary revisions? Keep in mind that there are always revisions; the key question is, are those revisions crucial? If so, make them. If not, let the goals rest.
- Keep in mind the following three key points when creating goals:
  - Goals require students to engage actively with course content in authoritative ways.
  - Goals provide measurable evidence of what students have or haven't achieved.
  - Goals engage students on a level that achieves our best hopes for them.

Step 2: Reexamine the structure you created in chapter 3. Are there any revisions that are obvious and necessary? If so, make them. If not, move on.

Step 3: (Please note: Depending on your course, you may not need to do both Steps 3 and 4.) Go back and look at the assignments and assessments you created in chapter 4. Choose one to four projects you think will help identify whether students are meeting your course goals. Remember the following:

- You should have enough major assessment methods to measure the things you care about and to ensure that no single method counts for an unreasonable percentage of the final grade.
- You need to balance the preceding point with the realities of your work load. You should not have so many major assessments that you're not able to return them to your students in a timely manner (e.g., within two weeks).
- For each major project, be sure to identify the
  - audience
  - purpose
  - genre
- Identify the related goals for each major project.

Step 4: Look at the revised exam questions you created in chapter 5.

- Make any obvious and necessary revisions or additions.
- If particular exam questions match up with particular units or sections of you new course structure, make that clear in your notes.
- When necessary for exam questions, be sure to identify the audience, purpose, and genre.
- Remember to think about the value of making meaning in contexts of uncertainty.
- Remember there is some room for content memorization, which can be achieved just as effectively with a small number of questions.

Step 5: Consider the pedagogical techniques you worked with in chapter 6. Remember, as you're adding them to your course or syllabus, to always align particular activities with particular assessments (which, in turn, are aligned with particular goals). In other words, we're all pressed for time so don't use a pedagogical activity or approach that you don't need no matter how interesting or engaging it seems. Chances are, if there's an approach you really like that doesn't fit your course, it will be appropriate for another course later on.

- First, jot down any semester-long exercise you may have developed to support a particular assignment (e.g., a series of mini essays or a series of increasingly difficult data sets). Be sure to think about the following:
  - How can this approach can be incorporated to ensure that students have repeated opportunities to practice key skills?
  - How can this approach can be incorporated at increasing levels of difficulty?

- ◦ Should this activity be *minimally graded, proportionally graded,* or *ungraded?*
- • Second, incorporate particular day-to-day or one-shot activities you developed at the end of chapter 6, whether adopted entirely from chapter 6 or developed on your own.
  - ◦ Situate these exercises in units, chapters, or sections of the course where they would be particularly useful or productive.
  - ◦ Be sure to designate whether they are minimally graded, proportionally graded, or ungraded.

Step 6: Set all of this work aside for two or three days but no more. Give yourself time to clear your head and get some perspective.

Step 7: Draft your syllabus, using the ideas provided here as a guide. Once done, set the syllabus aside for a day or two, then revise and proofread it.

# 7

## ASSESSING WICKEDNESS

This chapter is deliberately short for the following three reasons:

1. If you've followed the various steps in the previous chapters, the assessment plan for your course should already be set up.
2. This isn't a book about institutions, it's a book about courses.
3. If this chapter was longer, most people probably wouldn't read it.

### Course Assessment

The first point here comes from Barbara Tewksbury (B. Tewksbury, personal communication, May 19–22, 2008), who argues that one of the benefits of careful outcomes-based course design (also known as backward design) is that assessment "falls naturally" from a well-designed course. In other words, as long as you've been following the steps in this book, beginning with goals and proceeding through to assignments, you likely already have a tool for ensuring that your course is doing what you say it's doing.

Consider the following outcome from the philosophy class in chapter 2:

> By the end of the course, students will be able to articulate the value of Native American philosophies for contemporary life.

A goal like this leads very naturally to the following assignment:

> Construct a plan spanning at least the next 10 years of your life in which you incorporate Native American thinking into your everyday life. Be sure to cite and carefully analyze the complexities of at least three of the texts we've worked with this semester.

Or take this example in physics, also from chapter 2:

Goal: *Students will be able to distinguish between evidence and conclusions and evaluate the validity of the latter.*

Assignment: *Students will be able to analyze a contemporary scientific debate as portrayed in the media, distinguishing between evidence and conclusions and evaluating the validity of the latter.*

The following example is from sociology:

Goal: *Students will be able to analyze the implications of sociological theory for daily life.*

Exam question: *Using one major theory from our reading this unit, argue for the study of sociology in the training of one of the following fields: nurses, teachers, politicians.*

In each of these cases, well-written course goals lead very naturally to assignments or exam questions. This is great, because, well, that's assessment. Each of these assignments and the exam question provide information to the professor about how well the students can perform or meet the course goals. This is all we're trying to figure out when we're assessing something: Can our students do what we say they can do? If most of the students can, then clearly whatever methods we're using in the course are working well, and we should keep using them until our goals change or we get bored and start to explore new methods.

On the other hand, if a large percentage of the students can't complete the assignments or answer the questions in convincing ways, then we know that something isn't working in the course. Perhaps our expectations are too high or not communicated particularly effectively. Or perhaps we aren't preparing the students enough so they can achieve the kinds of complex tasks and thinking we want them to perform.

Regardless, the point is that because we've created at least some assignments and at least some exam questions that connect directly to our goals for our students, once students have completed those assignments and answered those questions, our assessment of that particular goal is essentially over. We now know what we need to know, and we can move on to other things. In this way, assessment is not some added step we have to squeeze into our busy schedules; it comes naturally from what we're already doing.

## Institutional Assessment

The second reason this chapter will be short is because this book is about courses, not about institutions. I've written elsewhere about institutional assessment, particularly about the need for integrity during any process that seeks to fulfill accreditation standards (Hanstedt, 2012). Here, my main concern is with what happens in our individual courses. Nevertheless, it's important to recognize the ways in which what occurs at the university level can affect our work with students. Figure 7.1 is a variation on the flowchart I introduced at the end of chapter 2 in Figure 2.6.

The basic idea behind this chart is that there is a connection between the broadest vision of the goals of the university, down through the various programs and colleges and departments and majors, and into individual courses. I've added a final step connecting course goals to the actual work students do in their courses. Key here is the fact that at an institution where assessment is working as it should, the arrows flow in both directions. That is, the institutional vision constructed at the highest levels informs what happens in our courses, and what happens in our courses informs the institutional vision. These arrows, therefore, indicate the dialogic nature of assessment done well.

This is important because it means that we should have some degree of control over what happens in our courses. Sometimes this may require some negotiation at the department or program level, but finally an assessment program that's really effective will take into account the smart work of faculty at the street level and bring that good work into the conversation. This is, of course, the best-case scenario.

If you find yourself in a less than best-case situation, where course outcomes are dictated from above, then the fallback is an approach discussed in chapter 2, where individuals align their high-end, idealistic, and authoritative goals with more generic departmental outcomes (see Figure 7.2).

**Figure 7.1.** University mission and its relation to our courses and assignments.

University Mission Statement

Institutional Student Learning Outcomes

Departmental Outcomes

Course Goals

Assignments, Exams, and So Forth

**Figure 7.2.** Aligning course goals with institutional goals in a less than ideal situation.

Institutional Outcomes

Students will be able to read, listen, and observe carefully.

Departmental Outcomes

Students will be able to apply apt methods in the analysis of literature.

Course Goals

Using close analysis, students will be able to argue for the value of poetry in the

contemporary world.

Understanding that the departmental and institutional outcomes are often defined broadly enough to allow a wide range of goals created by individual instructors is essential. The trick is to find a particular broad departmental outcome to align with our high-end, idealistic, and authoritative goals. Indeed, I would go so far as to say that if we're not in some way doing that, if we're simply importing the generic goals into our courses, then something is wrong.

Sometimes we develop goals for our individual courses that don't connect to the institutional or departmental goals. Assuming these goals aren't too off the charts, I think the fact that we have them is okay; it shows that we're thinking carefully about our work and our courses, that we're moving beyond received wisdom.

In situations like this, I suggest an also-and approach. First, be sure to include goals in your course that meet the desired outcomes required by your department and institution. Try to adapt these goals as much as possible to ensure that when they are implemented in your course, they are high end and engage students on an authoritative level.

Second, move beyond those goals to make sure your courses reflect your values, your knowledge, and the motivations that brought you to the field. Make sure these goals are high end and authoritative, but don't apologize for including material, ideas, and assignments that go beyond the lowest-common-denominator needs of the institution. Indeed, be aware that these goals often will energize you and make you a more engaged and engaging

**Figure 7.3** Including goals that go beyond university mission and departmental outcomes.

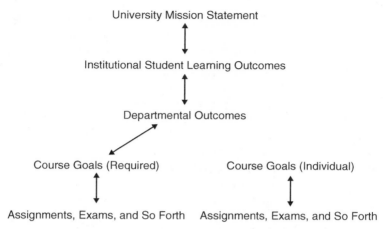

instructor. These goals can bring pleasure to your work, and that that pleasure will be passed along to your students.

What I'm envisioning, then, is a revised flow chart that looks something like Figure 7.3. The course goals and subsequent assignments on the left of this chart align with departmental and institutional goals; the results of students' work are reported up the food chain, to the department and beyond. The course goals and the assignments on the right, in contrast, are designed by the instructor to reflect his or her individual goals for the course and student learning in the field. The instructor uses the results of students' work on the assignments and exams to assess the effectiveness of student learning and to make changes to future iterations of the course to improve that learning.

My point, finally, is that just because some of our course goals come down to us from on high, that doesn't mean we're limited to those goals. We have the right in our own courses to have additional goals that reflect our own priorities in the field and our sense of how students best learn. These data never get reported to administrators, but that doesn't matter: that information is for us. It tells us how our students are doing and helps us improve our courses.

## Assessing Wickedness

Setting aside matters of institutional assessment, what if we simply want to know if all this is working, if our students really are developing the capacity to step into a complicated, messy world and interact with that world in thoughtful and productive ways?

On some level we recognize that authority is a lifelong project, an aptitude that builds over time. Movement in this area is difficult to measure in the context of a 14-week course or even over the course of 4 years of undergraduate education. But even so, is there any way we can get a sense of whether what we're doing in our courses is working?

What I'm about to offer is less of a definitive answer than the beginning of a conversation. Table 7.1 is a rubric developed by my former colleague, Kim Filer, now at Virginia Tech (Filer and Hanstedt, 2014). Filer developed this rubric to assess authority using the work of Marcia Baxter Magolda, combining some of Magolda's foundational ideas from early in her career with some of her more recent work.

Recall the pair of equations that are the basis for my theory of agency.

CONTENT KNOWLEDGE + SKILL KNOWLEDGE
= SENSE OF AUTHORITY

CONTENT KNOWLEDGE + SKILL KNOWLEDGE + SENSE
OF AUTHORITY = THOUGHTFUL CHANGE

TABLE 7.1
**The Authority Rubric**

|  | *Beginning* | *Emerging* | *Demonstrating* |
|---|---|---|---|
| Competence | Developing the foundational knowledge and skills in the discipline | Demonstrating consistent foundational knowledge and skills | Not intimidated by new competencies, to the point of actually seeking them out |
| Context | Focus is on individual ideas as interpreted through their own ideas and interpretations of the world around them | Showing understanding of ideas positioned in contexts (time, political, social) | Ability to transfer and adapt ideas into new and appropriate contexts |
| Authority | Reliance on external authority and sources | Actively working on constructing new ways of making meaning, including questioning self and others | Trusts the internal voice sufficiently to craft a philosophy —of life and of the field—and to contribute to the field and to society |

The first of these equations is crucial because it acknowledges that when we talk about authority what we want is an attitude based on learning. We're not interested in confidence or arrogance or even self-efficacy, all of which can be based on nothing. A person may be confident that he or she is good looking, even though by objective standards, the person really is not. A person can have a sense of efficacy in relation to parenting without ever having been responsible for a child. Authority, in contrast, grows out of learning and experience. It draws on content knowledge and skill knowledge.

The first row of Filer's rubric, labelled *Competence,* essentially gauges the student's knowledge. Does the paper or presentation in question demonstrate the student's understanding of the field? The second row in the rubric labeled *Context* builds on this: Has the student moved beyond opinion into an understanding of larger contexts that may shape a problem? Does the student understand the big picture?

The third row, *Authority,* relates to the second equation that results in thoughtful change. What we're after is not mindless or uneducated change, but thoughtful, deliberate, informed responses to complex problems that need to be addressed. This equation is essentially the wicked student in action, the student with content and skill but also with a sense of authority. The student has the capacity to dive into the unknown and respond to complex problems using the knowledge and skills learned in the course and measured in the first two rows of Filer's rubric. In its simplest form, then, the first two rows of Table 7.1 rubric have to do with student mastery of learning, whereas the third line has to do with measuring their sense of authority.

Because authority, content, and skill are intertwined, however, what we see in this rubric is also a movement, even in the first two rows of Table 7.1, toward authority. As students move from the Emerging column to the Demonstrating column in both Competence and Context, we begin to see elements that relate to wickedness: a willingness to face new challenges and the ability to transfer knowledge from one area to another. Consequently, Table 7.1 has the capacity to reveal an increase in authority (or not) in students in not one but two ways.

To demonstrate, let's use a few small excerpts of student work. The first is from a creative writing student early in his career. Prompted to reflect on ideas he'd developed as a result of being in this course, he wrote, "The nature of poetry can be humorous and can use low-brow humor to convey a message or lesson. I used specific line-breaks to help show what I learned over the semester."

That this was all the student had to say tells us a great deal. The only reference to learned knowledge after an entire semester in the course has to do with line breaks. In terms of competence, this passage is clearly at the beginning level of the rubric. Context is also relatively low. That poetry can be humorous is not a new idea. That this student wasn't aware of that probably puts him at the beginning level.

Paradoxically, this student's willingness to attempt an argument about what poetry can do, where it could go, probably pushes him toward emerging when it comes to authority. Unaware of the fact that what he's proposing is not new, he's nonetheless willing to attempt something that he sees as different. Finally, though, it's clear he's not particularly far along in his development in any of these areas.

Compare this to Nathan, an international relations major who created a portfolio his senior year. He wrote the following when asked to introduce a piece of his academic work:

> For this paper I was asked to identify a theoretical lens of international politics and explore an international crisis through this lens. For an International Relations major this is a typical assignment. What made this paper challenging was incorporating the global economic system and finding economic motivations for political actions.
>
> Because this was a new approach, I started by heavily researching the economic background for Russian, the European Union, the United States, and Ukraine. I sought out expert analysis on the economies of these actors and from there built a basis for incorporating political analysis.
>
> This assignment left several questions for future research and observation: Will Russia continue with aggressive actions in Ukraine? How does the conflict in Syria play into Russia's future plans?
>
> This paper is representative of what I enjoy and why I chose this major. I hope to expand my analytical skills in order to better reason motivations for political actions and predict future behavior.

The contrast between this passage and the previous one is as different as night and day. In terms of competence, Nathan clearly understands not just the foundational knowledge—his chosen theoretical lens—but the foundational skills. He knows what he needs to research to be able to apply that lens. At the very least, he's at the emerging stage in this area and most likely in demonstrating. Because of his comment that this is what he enjoys, as well as his future research questions, it seems safe to assume that he's willing and capable of going beyond what he's done in this paper and seeking new competencies.

He also performs well in terms of context: The very nature of the assignment asks him to recognize how different lenses relate to different situations. It goes without saying that this is an essential skill in international relations, where change is constant and grounded in recent and ancient history. Of course, because we're only looking at his introduction to the essay, as opposed to the essay itself, we're limited in how thoroughly we can judge his effectiveness in this area. An instructor assessing the full portfolio, in contrast, would have access to both the introduction and the essay, and wouldn't face these limitations.

Because we are only looking at this one sample of his work here, it's also difficult to judge the degree to which, in terms of authority, he has crafted a philosophy of life and can contribute to his field and society. Nonetheless, we see indications that he may be demonstrating his competency in those last two paragraphs. His rhetorical questions indicate that he's comfortable moving beyond the known into the unknown, asking what's next, and how this relates to the future or to other situations. His final statement about predicting future behavior indicates a desire to shift from an analysis of current situations to a prediction of future situations. In other words, he wants to add something to both his own learning and to what that learning can bring to the larger conversation.

Our application of this rubric is limited by my decision for reasons of time and space to include only introductory writing instead of actual student artifacts. Many of the questions in this discussion are answered when we look at the actual work of the students. Additionally, I'm presenting a fairly obvious contrast between a student at the beginning of his academic career and one who is about to graduate. Is it safe to assume there's going to be some development over the course of four years? Sadly, no. Arum and Roksa (2011) pointed out that nearly half of university students demonstrate little or no growth in critical thinking and complex reasoning, and that these shortcomings fall disproportionately on the culturally and economically disadvantaged. Put another way, we're past the time when we can assume that learning and growth just happen. They don't. We need to be deliberate about what we do in our classrooms. We need to be thoughtful about our approaches. We need to find ways to ensure that every student moves from beginning to demonstrating in competence and context, yes, but also in authority.

Finally, it's worth noting that nothing says that authority needs its own rubric. Table 7.2 is a variation on a rubric for assessing the stories and poems of creative writing students.

In the previous iteration of this rubric, the column that currently qualifies a student story or poem as *strong* was the highest assessment a student could achieve. All of the elements described in the strong column essentially had to do with mastery of style, structure, and so on, and were considered the best a student could do. This is a little peculiar if you think about it, because most works of literary significance receive attention because they

**TABLE 7.2**

**Assessing Authority in Student Stories And Poems**

| | Basic | Beginning | Strong | Excellent |
|---|---|---|---|---|
| Style | Struggles to control language in terms of grammar, proofreading, and basic sentence structure | Competent in use of language in terms of grammar and proofreading but also with an emerging sense of how language can be used to express more than mere denotation | Beyond competence, a suitable style involves accurate and expressive sentence structures | Uses word choice and syntax to develop new, thoughtful, and effective means of expression |
| Structure | Very basic or obvious structures or use of a structure that has very little impact on meaning, content, and emotion; form and function have no obvious relationship | Occasional moments where structural choices help to convey use of structure to aid in conveying meaning, content, and emotion | Full development and structural integrity in relation of the parts to the whole; beginning, middle, and end (along with subordinate parts) must be fully developed and sequenced in expressive relation to one another | Adapts structural forms or creates new structural forms as an effective means of better conveying content, meaning, and emotion |
| Elements of craft | Uses various elements of craft inconsistently or unevenly; very little balance of the elements in terms of their relation to genre, purpose, or meaning | Occasionally uses some elements of craft well, but use is inconsistent; other elements may be used poorly, or the balance between elements is counter to the needs of genre, purpose, and meaning | Mastery of a genre's craft elements, also demonstrates an appropriate balance among these elements in terms of conveying a work's overall purpose or meaning | Uses elements of craft in original and innovative ways that increase the overall effectiveness of the work |
| Significant content | Appears to pay very little attention to meaning and purpose, focusing instead on superficial plot or message | Attempts to say something but does so in a clichéd or pedantic way | Seeks to say something meaningful, working in the service of curiosity, insight, and courage | Makes a point that hasn't been made before, or renders an idea in a new and invigorating way |

in some way go beyond mastery, beyond what's already being done. They bring us voices or structures of characters or ideas that we haven't encountered before. Even stale detective stories try to provide some twist to grab our attention. If this is what we hope our students will be able to achieve after they graduate, why are we not assessing this while they are in our classes?

The far right-hand column in Table 7.2 adds that additional layer—looking at students' work not just in terms of mastering what's come before but of what students are adding to the conversation. Are they striving to say something new or say something in a new way? Are they moving beyond what they've been taught about structure and creating new forms for a new age?

Of course, we do not expect every student to hit that level of *excellent*, not even some seniors. Nor do we assume that because they *don't* reach that far right column, they won't necessarily get an "A" in the course. Assumptions along these lines vastly oversimplify the purpose of assessment, which is more about strengthening the program than assigning grades. The point, in the end, is that if that fourth column encapsulates our best hopes for our students, we need to include it as part of our assessment process. How else will we know if our students are where we want them to be?

It may be tempting to say that all of this is more appropriate in fields like creative writing. After all, isn't being creative by definition about moving beyond? However, in talking to colleagues in fields ranging from physics to history to  psychology, it's become clear to me that the students professors most admire are those who somehow, on some small level, in some small way, have learned to add to the conversations of our fields. Most often, these are our superstars, our honors students, and our academic overachievers. Which is fine. But given the world we're living in, where the Internet is filled with misinformation and talking heads on news channels who don't even worry about the facts; where half the country seems armed to the teeth, and the other half is vehemently opposed to violence; where technology and climate change and globalism and the economy are changing so rapidly that we can't anticipate the morning's headlines from one day to the next—in such a world we need to instill a level of authority not just in our best students but in all the students in all our fields.

# CONCLUSION

A s I mentioned in chapter 1, I'm aware that what I'm presenting here can easily come off as formulaic, even uncompromising: Follow Step 1, follow Step 2, then voilà, we have a world full of perfect college graduates. Education doesn't work like that, of course. Students are complex beings, driven by varying, sometimes contradictory, sometimes even self-defeating motives. They have lives beyond the classroom with jobs, families, clubs, and love affairs. We're relatively incidental to their world. And much of the culture beyond our classrooms works hard to send students messages about values and learning and self-worth that don't mesh with the presumptions behind this book. Fair enough. Still, though, I contend that if we're not doing our best to send an alternative message about self and self-worth and the potential of all students to shape and reshape the world in thoughtful, productive ways, then the world might end up in pretty bad shape.

Of course, we academics are complex as well. Although we share many traits—an appreciation for the life of the mind, a strong desire for autonomy—we're nonetheless very different. What works for one professor in the classroom might not work for another; assignments that achieve profound outcomes in one field might not work in the next.

All of this in mind, I like to end these conversations with four cautions. When designing or redesigning a course, when adding new pedagogies, when creating new assessments, please keep the following in mind:

1. *Do not overwhelm yourself.* There are a lot of good ideas out there. As our understanding of the brain and how students actually learn advance, more thoughtful and effective approaches to teaching are being developed every day. It's an exciting time to be a professor. Keep in mind, it's not necessary to bring all these approaches into your classroom at once. Doing so can often be exhausting for the professor and students. Take your time and introduce a few new approaches gradually. Once you've got them established and you feel comfortable with them, then bring in others.

2. *Adapt teaching techniques to your own style.* You know who you are as an instructor. You know how you wish to present yourself and which presentations of your instructorly self seem to work best in the classroom. Feel free to choose approaches that match your strengths and to adapt approaches to compensate for some of your weaknesses. Gender, race, body size, and age all have an impact on classroom dynamics. Keep that in mind when designing courses and choosing pedagogies.

3. That said, *be sure to take a few risks.* Push your boundaries. Do so because that's how we learn and grow; do so because that's how we want our students to learn and grow, and we need to model that for them; and do so because teaching the same old thing semester after semester will get stale. And if it's stale for you, it'll be stale for the students. And that will have a negative impact on their learning.

4. *Tinker.* You will bomb. There will be failures. These will range from moments that just feel awkward to moments that feel like the classroom has imploded. That's normal. Change, growth, development, whatever you want to call it, involves stumbling, for both us and our students. For many, the first impulse after a failure is to just drop the exercise or assignment or design and go back to the way things were. Don't do that. Instead, step back, examine, and think about what exactly went wrong and how adjustments might be made. Then make them and try again. If you bomb four times, then fine, just drop it; but until then, consider, adjust, try again, and learn something new. This way of thinking is what we want for and from our students. We need to model it for them.

In the end, if you use nothing else from this book, if all the activities, the assignments, or those weird exam questions just don't work for you, at the very least, please take away with you the following points.

First, we are facing a student culture that has been tested to death. This history has many consequences, but the most important for our purposes is that it's led students to believe that education and learning begin and end with the memorization of facts and formulas. Certainly mastery of content is crucial in every field, but this is not an either-or situation. We also need students who can approach new content that they haven't seen before, who are capable of learning how to learn and can develop formulas and algorithms to address problems that don't even exist yet. We need wicked students. We need wicked graduates. We need wicked citizens, wicked neighbors, wicked businesses, wicked clergy, wicked teachers. It's as simple as that. We must prepare our students for a complex world.

Second, we must be deliberate in designing our courses and be as thought-ful with them as we are with our own research and scholarship. We must acknowledge that what worked for us as undergraduates likely won't work for most of our students. For one thing, this generation of students is different. But more importantly, most of our students aren't like us, aren't intrinsically invested in the life of the mind or inclined to pursue advanced degrees in a narrowly focused field in order to become professors. This isn't good or bad, but it is a fact: We're weird. So we need to be thoughtful about how to bring the weird joy we find in our weird fields to students so that they too can find pleasure in the beautiful problems that fascinate us.

Exactly how you do these two things—create wicked students and be deliberate about how you design your courses—is entirely up to you. But they have to be done. My hope is that this book will at the very least move you forward in your thinking about these matters. If indeed it does, please let me know. I'd like to hear about the methods you develop, the things that work, and those that don't. Because in the end, we're all in this together.

# POSTER PROJECT
# FOR ENGLISH 322:
# COMPOSITION THEORY
# AND PRACTICE

Assignment:

This assignment has two parts: with a group, you must develop a literacy project for a population of your choice and present it in poster form. Individually, you must write a rationale that explains the reasoning behind the project your group developed.

Due Dates:

Tuesday, 11 March—E-mail me by 1:00 with the names of your group members

Tuesday, 18 March—Bring to class a project proposal, prepared by the group, listing

- The population you're working with
- The angle you hope to take with your project
- A list of three sources from our reading that you will likely use
- A list of three additional sources from outside research that you will likely use

Tuesday, 8 April—Polished draft of the poster, to be presented to the class. Last day for a conference at the writing center with a complete draft of your individual rationale

Tuesday, 15 April—Polished draft of individual rationales, four copies

Thursday, 17 April—Peer responding

Thursday, 17 April—Poster presentations in Colket Center over the lunch hour

Monday, 21 April—Final rationale (at the start of class)

## *The Literacy Project*

For this portion of the assignment, you must prepare a poster that outlines an approach to improving the writing abilities of a particular population. Exactly which population you choose is entirely up to you, but the more specific you are in defining that audience (e.g., first-year students at Roanoke College as opposed to first-year students in general; the homeless in Washington, DC as opposed to the homeless everywhere/anywhere) the easier it will be to research this audience and to develop your project.

Once you've chosen a population, you are to develop a literacy program that will meet them where they are and improve their writing. Exactly what you develop is also up to you. On your poster you should outline *at least* the following:

- the major components/assignments of the program
- the process/support features you will include to enable the population to meet the program goals
- the instructor's role relative to offering feedback/assessment/coaching, and so on

Your posters will be presented to the Roanoke College community on the last Thursday of the semester (see syllabus) over the lunch hour. As with any formal academic poster presentation, you will be expected to stand by your posters in order to explain the program you have proposed, as well as the thinking behind it. Assume very little—or even no—expertise with regard to writing issues on the part of your audience.

Groups should consist of two to three people; those who wish may petition to allow a fourth person into a group, or to do the project on their own, though the latter is highly discouraged.

Though what ultimately matters is the success of your program as a whole, please know that I will be paying particular attention to

- The complexity of the ideas you present
- Your familiarity with the strengths and weaknesses of the various schools of thought and approaches to writing pedagogies that we've discussed all semester
- Your willingness and/or ability to take some innovative risks, to push our thinking about how best to teach people to write

- The effectiveness and professionalism of your presentation, with regard both to the poster, and to your ability to articulate orally the benefits and rationales of your program

## *The Rationale*

Individually, each of you will be asked to write a rationale justifying the literacy program your group developed. Though your group will of course share some of the ideas behind the program, these rationales should be written entirely on your own.

Essentially, these rationales are research papers. They should demonstrate that you know your audience, that you're familiar with and have given careful consideration to the ideas we've been discussing all semester, and that you've gone out and done some serious scholarly research that goes beyond the reading we've done in class.

All sources—both those from class and those from your own research—must be cited properly.

Though what finally matters is the success of the rationale as a whole, please know that I will be paying particular attention to

- Your ability to give the rationale some cohesive focus—call it a thesis, if you wish—so that it does not become simply a string of isolated factoids, each relating to a portion of your project without relating to one another
- Your ability to articulate the complexity of the ideas and practices you are presenting—in other words, simple answers will not be accepted
- Your thoughtful use of materials from our reading this semester
- Your ability to find appropriate and useful outside sources to support your arguments

# TRAVEL FILM ASSIGNMENT FOR FIRST-YEAR SEMINAR ON TRAVEL LITERATURE

INQ 110: First-Year Seminar: Other Places

### *Major Project*

Assignment

This assignment has two parts: with a group, you must develop a short film that serves as a public service announcement to students who are going to study abroad. Individually, you must write a researched rationale that justifies the arguments you make in your film.

Due Dates:

Monday, 31 October—E-mail me by 1:00 with the names of your group members, along with your group's topic.

Sunday, 13 November—No later than midnight, post to your group ePortfolio page an annotated bibliography of the two scholarly sources you will contribute to your group's research. Please note: there must be NO overlaps in the articles each person contributes to the group. Also note: everyone in the group should have read ALL of the articles by class on Tuesday, 15 November.

Thursday, 17 November: Linked to your ePortfolio by 7:30 a.m.: a complete draft of your study abroad public service announcement film.

Monday, 21 November—First draft of individual rationales, including all sources—posted to your ePortfolio and in the mailbox outside my office by no later than 10 A.M.

Tuesday, 29 November—Linked to your ePortfolio by 7:30 a.m.: a revised draft of your study abroad public service announcement film.

Tuesday, 6 December—Polished draft of individual papers, four copies.
Thursday, 8 December—Peer response session. Attendance mandatory.
Monday, 12 December—Final drafts of paper due no later than 11 a.m.,
   in the box outside my door AND posted to your ePortfolio. Final
   drafts of films linked/posted to your ePortfolio no later than 4 p.m.

## *The Movie Project*

For this portion of the assignment, you must prepare a short (four to seven
minutes) film that serves as a public service announcement for students
who are about to study abroad. This film must deal with one of these three
periods:

* Before they leave
* While they are abroad
* Upon their return

Your goal is to give your audience informed advice that will help them
maximize the benefits of their time abroad. If you wish, you may choose to
further focus your film by addressing a particular audience—say, women,
science majors, and so on.

Key points:

* These films should have a clear thesis that drives the entire project. In
  other words, there should be some focus to your advice—I don't want
  15 random ideas that have nothing to do with each other.
* Further, the advice you give MUST evolve from: a) our reading
  this semester; and b) careful research into the scholarship of
  international education. Just to be clear, your scholarly sources
  must come from peer-reviewed academic journals written *by* highly
  educated scholars *for* highly educated scholars. No Google. No
  Yahoo. No newspapers or blogs, not even the *New York Times* or the
  *Wall Street Journal*.
* Films should have a careful balance between the literature and the
  outside scholarship. Overreliance upon one or the other will impact
  the final grade.
* These films should be pitched to an audience of your peers—people
  your age, who have *not* taken this class—and will be posted on
  YouTube. I'd strongly encourage you to think about using humor,
  music, images, and so on, to engage this audience. In addition, you

may use stories drawn from our reading to illustrate your points (though these readings will not count as your scholarly sources).

Groups should consist of three to four people from our class;
Though what ultimately matters is the success of your film as a whole, please know that I will be paying particular attention to:

- The complexity of the ideas you present
- Your ability to incorporate appropriate scholarly research
- Your willingness and/or ability to take some innovative risks, to push our thinking about travel beyond the obvious
- The effectiveness and professionalism of your presentation
- Your effectiveness in appealing to a YouTube audience

## *The Individual Rationale*

Assignment:
Your assignment is to provide justification for your film project. Why did you provide the advice you did? How do you connect that advice with the readings and discussions we've been having all semester long? Why is this advice appropriate for your particular audience? For the particular segment (before, during, after) of the study abroad process that you chose?

You are writing these papers to me, your professor. Modify tone and choose appropriate evidence accordingly.

A few things to keep in mind:

- Make sure your essay has a clear, driving thesis. Relate everything in the paper back to the thesis. While this rationale has multiple parts, all of them, ultimately, should create a coherent essay.
- This is the final paper for this course. Show me that you know what you're talking about, that you're able to think about these matters in ways that go well beyond the average person. More particularly, I'm looking for:
  - Insightful ideas: new ways of thinking that go beyond our reading and discussions
  - Complexity of thought: avoiding simple answers
  - The ability to choose good sources, sources that really matter to you, and to use them effectively—that is, letting your sources serve your ideas, not the other way around.
- As you build your argument, I'm also looking for careful reading and analysis of both the class texts AND your outside sources. Give quotes.

Explain how you draw conclusions from those quotes by pointing to key words. Be sure to give enough context around your quotes so that the unfamiliar reader will understand.

- As with every other paper we've had this semester, these rationales should have good paragraphing (single idea, nice topic sentence), effective overall organization, good intros and conclusions, and careful proofreading.

## The Annotated Bibliography

In order to ensure that everyone is capable of reading a complex scholarly article—*and* contributing to the success of their group—each student is required to search for, read carefully, and annotate *two* appropriately academic articles from the field of international education that they feel will be useful to their group project.

This bibliography should be posted to your group's ePortfolio page no later than midnight on Sunday, 13 November. The annotated bibliography should contain the following information for *each* of the articles you found and read:

- An appropriate bibliography citation using MLA format. (See Hacker, *A Writer's Reference*, beginning on page 422)
- A brief paragraph summarizing the content of the article
- A brief paragraph explaining why you feel this article will be beneficial to the project. Go into some detail here, referring to particular passages or ideas in the article

# RESEARCH POSTER ASSIGNMENT FOR OCCUPATIONAL THERAPY

*Diane Parham*

## Evidence-Based Practice Poster Instructions

### *Creating Your Poster: Mandatory Requirements*

1. Poster materials

   Your poster should be presented on a standard trifold poster or project display board that is approximately 36" high and about 48" wide when opened up. By using a folded display board, you can easily display your poster on a tabletop. It is strongly recommended that you use display board material that is semi-rigid, as in foam board or corrugated board, so that it can support itself upright on a table without blowing over or collapsing. The background of the poster board can be any color that you choose.

2. Putting your poster together

   a. Your poster will consist of printouts that are arranged in an appealing fashion on your display board and firmly attached to the board.

   b. The center panel of your trifold poster will contain the title and research question. These should be in larger font than the rest of the poster, so that they are eye-catching and easy to read from far away. The center panel may also contain other content.

   c. The rest of the poster should present content in a logical sequence, reading from top to bottom on left panel, then top to bottom of right panel.

   d. All printouts attached to the poster should be typewritten using no smaller than 16-point font to assure easy reading for attendees.

   e. You may develop your poster using word processing documents or PowerPoint slides that add color and a design element to the poster. If you are so inclined, you may design your poster to have sections of your poster custom printed to allow for very large font sizes or other special features (note that this may require you to pay for commercial photocopying services).

f.  Strive to make a visually appealing poster that will draw the interest of attendees. Beyond required components, you may choose to add pictures or graphics to your poster that convey what your topic is about.

g.  Do not forget to add YOUR NAME to the poster. This should go on the center panel somewhere under the title and/or research question.

3.  Required components

a.  Title. Your title should be located at the top of the CENTER section of the trifold display. It should be brief (no more than 20 words) and *capture the major issue or findings* of your research, such as, "Animal-Assisted Therapy May Help Alleviate Depression in Elders," "Tai Chi Is More Effective than Balance Training in Preventing Falls Among the Elderly," "Is Sensory Integration Intervention Helpful for Children with Autism?" or "Warning: Single Session Therapy for PTSD May Be Harmful."

b.  Research Question. Clearly and prominently present your research question so attendees' attention will be drawn to it. This usually is placed in the CENTER section, under the title.

c.  Search Strategy: Provide a brief synopsis of the search strategy that you used to find your five articles, including key words, the databases that you searched, and your criteria for including or excluding studies.

d.  Major Findings. Your major findings sections should consist of summaries of a minimum of five research studies published in peer-reviewed journals. Each study should be independently and briefly summarized and be of direct relevance to your clinical question. Summarize BRIEFLY each study using the appropriate matrix used in this class (Quantitative Research, Single-Subject Research, or Qualitative Research). You don't have much space to accomplish this, so include *only the most important information on the matrix*, and word it *concisely*. Also you may revise the matrices by merging headings, if that works for you—as long as the critical information is there, and it is easy for readers to distinguish between studies.

Organizing the matrices on your poster:

○  If your research question addresses effectiveness of an intervention, but you could only find one or a few articles that examined this intervention, and the rest are studies providing background information—don't worry, that is fine! In this case, organize the matrices on your poster so that it is clear to the reader *which studies directly addressed your research question, versus studies that provide background or related information.* If all of your studies directly addressed your research question, then fine, you do not need to make separate categories (but see further instructions next . . .)

○ On the poster, order the matrices within each category in *descending order of level of evidence,* so that the study with the highest level of evidence is at the top, the next highest is below it, and so on. If two or more studies tie at the same level of evidence, then order them alphabetically by the last name of the first author.

e. Implications for Evidence-Based Practice

This part of your poster session should answer the question, "So what?—What difference does this research make in clinical decision-making?" In other words, now that you have studied these articles, how should their findings, all together, best be used to guide clinical practice with respect to your clinical question? This component should be written in a narrative format, though it is okay to use bullets to emphasize major points. The following are suggested questions that might help you to develop specific implications for evidence-based practice:

i. What SPECIFIC interventions in occupational therapy do these studies support or NOT support?

ii. Given the levels of evidence of these research studies, with how much confidence can you draw conclusions about practice from them?

iii. To which populations might findings from the studies be generalized or NOT generalized?

iv. If you were in clinical practice in an area related to your poster, how would your knowledge of these studies, taken all together, influence decisions you might make about using the intervention for particular people? Given your knowledge, is there any way you can identify who might be a good candidate versus not so good candidate for this intervention?

v. How might the knowledge that you have gained be used to guide practice policies in the workplace or in public health?

vi. What gaps in knowledge exist, as related to your clinical question? What do we still NOT know that would be important to find out, in order to answer your clinical question?

## *References*

Provide complete references for articles referred to in your poster, using APA style. If you need room on your poster, you may print your references using a smaller font for the poster, or create a separate handout of references.

## Orally Presenting Your Poster: Mandatory Requirements

1. Oral Presentation
   You should be prepared to provide a brief overview, no more than five minutes in length, of the main points of your poster to attendees.
2. Skill in Answering Questions
   You should be prepared to answer the questions of attendees regarding your poster. For instance, the course instructor or other attendees may ask you to go more in-depth on your search strategy, on one or more of the articles that you have summarized, or on how you came up with your implications for practice.

## Evaluation of Your Poster Session

You will be able to earn a maximum of 100 points on your poster session. Your session will be evaluated on the basis of the (a) depth of thought, thoroughness, accuracy, specificity, and/or credibility of each required component; (b) quality of writing; (c) neatness, organization, visual appeal, and creativity of the poster; and (d) effectiveness in communicating major points and ability to answer questions. The course instructor will award points as follows:

Descriptiveness of title (5 points)
Clarity of research question (5 points)
Clarity and credibility of search strategy (5 points)
Relevance of reviewed research to student's clinical question (5 points)
Summaries of reviewed research (25 points)
Implications for evidence-based practice (20 points)
Quality of writing (10 points)
Neatness, visual appeal, and creativity of poster (10 points)
Oral presentation of poster and ability to answer questions (15 points)

# FINAL EXAM TAKE-HOME QUESTION ON WHAT MATTERS

## Study Guide for Final Exam

Part 1: Take-home (40%–50%)
This section of the exam is due upon your arrival for the final exam on Thursday, 24 April, at 8:30 a.m. It must be typewritten and double-spaced.

Assignment:
I want you to write about one thing that you figured out in this class that *matters*. It could be something about the teaching of writing, something about the nature of language, something about yourself, something about humanity, something about how to live life or about knowing oneself or about working with others or about baking brownies . . .

In short, I don't care what it is that "matters," as long as it truly *does* matter to you.

I do require that:

- Whatever you choose to write about must demonstrate a thoughtful approach to the readings and discussions we've had this semester.
- You cite *at least* three readings we've explored this semester.

You make sure that your essay has a clear and focused thesis backed up by very specific and well-analyzed references, paraphrases, and quotations from our texts. Get as specific as humanly possible when discussing the details!

# MINI-GROUP ESSAY ASSIGNMENT FOR ENGLISH 338: VICTORIAN LITERATURE

## Group Projects

### *Assignment:*

1. On group project days, each member of the group should come to class with a specific question about *one* particular work from that day's reading.

2. As a group, quickly choose a question that you find interesting and that you feel is significant to a more general understanding of the work and to the course as a whole.

3. Discuss the question among yourselves and arrive, at least tentatively, at a thesis—an answer—that is well supported by carefully analyzed textual evidence.

4. Each time the group meets, *everyone* in the group should take careful notes of the discussion. *At least two people* for each session should be assigned the task of synthesizing these notes into a coherent, one- to two-page single-spaced typed essay, to be turned in to my mailbox by the time listed on the syllabus. The recorders should be certain to list their names in the upper-left-hand corner of the summary, followed by the names of each group member who attended class that day, and to turn in a Group Project Log with the finished paper. Group members who are not in class for a group session should not be listed on the mini-essay and will receive an F for that particular session grade. *Each member of the group must share recording responsibilities at some point during the semester.*

5. Once I hand back annotated copies of the essays, it is the job of the recorders to get copies to each member of the group as soon as possible.

A few odds and ends:

- In order for these projects to work, everyone in the group must carry their weight. In order to ensure that this happens, reading quizzes will be given on group project days. Should an individual fail a quiz (fewer than 6 out of 10 points), he or she will have one full grade taken from the group grade. Should this same individual fail a second quiz, he or she will lose two full grades. A third quiz failure will lead to dismissal from the class. Similarly, if the project logs make it evident that a particular student is not carrying his or her weight with the group, action will be taken.

- Beyond that, keep in mind that these small group sessions can work extremely well, particularly if we all recognize that this is an opportunity to learn from one another, to share each other's strengths. This requires some effort on everybody's part: If you're quiet, speak up. If you're a know-it-all or a grade monger (and you know who you are!), just stay calm and listen to the input of others—nothing can destroy the effectiveness of these projects more than one individual taking over. Whatever happens, *respect one another's opinions.* If you find yourselves at odds with each other, see that as an opportunity to move forward—you don't have to agree with each other, but you should come to see the ways in which your differences of opinion enrich our understanding of the material.

# GROUP LOG FOR MINI-GROUP ESSAYS

## Group Project Log

Project #:

Group Members:

Recorders:

## Group Meetings Outside of Class (if any):

Date:           People who attended:

Date:           People who attended:

Date:           People who attended:

A draft of the project was distributed to the group on the following date:

Feedback to this draft was received from the following members:

In person:

By telephone:

Via e-mail/text:

In writing:

We, the undersigned, verify that the above is true (signature of recorders):

# REFERENCES

Ambrose, S., Bridges, M. W., DiPietro, M., Lovett, M. C., & Norman, M. K. (2010). *How learning works: Seven research-based principles for smart teaching.* San Francisco, CA: Jossey-Bass.

Anson, C. (2001). *The WAC casebook: Scenes from faculty reflection and program development.* New York, NY: Oxford University Press.

Association of American Colleges & Universities. (2015). *The LEAP challenge: Education for a world of unscripted problems.* Washington, DC: Author.

Arum, R., & Roksa, J. (2011). *Academically adrift: Limited learning on college campuses.* Chicago, IL: University of Chicago Press.

Bahls, P. (2012). *Student writing in the quantitative disciplines: A guide for college faculty.* San Francisco, CA: Jossey-Bass.

Barkley, E. (2010). *Student engagement techniques: A handbook for college faculty.* San Francisco, CA: Jossey-Bass.

Barkley, E. F., Cross, K. P., and Major, C. H. (2005). *Collaborative learning techniques: A handbook for college faculty.* San Francisco, CA: Jossey-Bass.

Bass, R. (2014, January). *Catalyst for change? Reframing ePortfolios in an evolving educational landscape.* Paper presented at the annual meeting of the Association of American Colleges & Universities, Washington, DC.

Baxter Magolda, M. (1999). *Creating contexts for learning and self-authorship: Constructive-developmental pedagogy.* Nashville, TN: Vanderbilt University Press.

Baxter Magolda, M. (2001). *Making their own way: Narrative for transforming higher education to promote self-development.* Sterling, VA.

Bean, J. (2011). *Engaging ideas.* San Francisco, CA: Jossey-Bass.

Berlin, J. (1988). Rhetoric and ideology in the writing class. *College English, 50,* 477–494.

Bloom, B. S. (Ed.). (1956). *Taxonomy of educational objectives: The classification of educational goals, by a committee of college and university examiners.* New York, NY: Longmans, Green.

Blumberg, P. (2009). *Developing learning-centered teaching: A practical guide for faculty.* San Francisco, CA: Jossey-Bass.

Deneen, C., & Hanstedt, P. (2011, June). *On the edge of the immeasurable: Utilizing the tension between idealism and measurability in course design.* Paper presented at the annual International Conference of the Humanities, Granada, Spain.

Diamond, R. M. (2008). *Designing and assessing courses and curricula* (3rd ed.). San Francisco, CA: Jossey-Bass.

Filer, K., & Hanstedt, P. (2014, July). *ePortfolios and whole person education: Exploring writing, identity, and efficacy*. Paper presented at a meeting of the Association for Authentic, Experiential, and Evidence-Based Learning, Boston, MA.

Fink, L. D. (2013). *Creating significant learning experiences: An integrated approach to designing college courses*. San Francisco, CA: Jossey-Bass.

Gardiner, L. F. (2008), Examples of outcome statements. In R. M. Diamond (Ed.), *Designing and assessing courses and curricula* (3rd ed., pp. 360–362). San Francisco, CA: Jossey-Bass.

Hanstedt, P. (2012). *General education essentials: A guide for college faculty*. San Francisco, CA: Jossey-Bass.

Kole, J. A., & Healy, A. (2007). Using prior knowledge to minimize interference when learning large amounts of information. *Memory & Cognition, 35*, 124–137.

Krathwohl, D. R. (2002). A revision of Bloom's taxonomy: An overview. *Theory into Practice, 41*, 212–218.

Kuh, G. (2008), *High-impact educational practices: What they are, who has access to them, and why they matter*. Washington, DC: Association of American Colleges & Universities.

Maki, P. (2010). Assessment. In P. L. Gaston (Ed.), *General education and liberal learning: Principles of effective practice*, 45–50. Washington, DC: Association of American Colleges & Universities.

Napier, S. J. (2005). *Anime from* Akira *to* Howl's moving castle*: Experiencing contemporary Japanese animation*. New York, NY: St. Martin's Griffin.

Reacting to the past. (2017). Retrieved from reacting.barnard.edu

Sandler, K. S. (1998). *Reading the rabbit: Explorations in Warner Bros. animation*. New Brunswick, NJ: Rutgers University Press.

Stoddart, R. M., & McKinley, M. J. (2006). Using narrative, literature, and primary sources to teach introductory psychology: An interdisciplinary approach. In D. S. Dunn & S. L. Chew (Eds.), *Best practices for teaching introduction to psychology* (pp. 111–128). Mahwah, NJ: Erlbaum.

Tewksbury, B. J., & Macdonald, R. H. (2017). *Cutting edge course design tutorial*. Retrieved from https://serc.carleton.edu/NAGTWorkshops/coursedesign/tutorial/TOC.html.

Student learning outcomes. (n.d.). Retrieved from http://www2.tulane.edu/liberal-arts/upload/Student_Learning_Outcomes.pdf

Tiu, F. S., & Osters, S. (2005). *Writing measureable learning outcomes*. Paper presented at the annual Texas A & M Assessment Conference, College Station.

Vargas, S., & Hanstedt, P. (2014). Exploring alternatives to the teaching of lab report writing: The portfolio method. *Double Helix, 1*(7, 11).

Wiggins, G., & McTighe, J. (2005). *Understanding by design*. Columbus, OH: Pearson.

Zull, J. (2002). *The art of changing the brain*. Sterling, VA: Stylus.

# ABOUT THE AUTHOR

Paul Hanstedt is the director of pedagogical innovation at Roanoke College, where he led the revision of a campus-wide general education program, developed an innovative writing-across-the-curriculum program, and taught a wide range of courses. He is the recipient of several teaching awards, including a 2013 State Council for Higher Education in Virginia Outstanding Faculty Award and the 2014 CASE Carnegie Virginia Professor of the Year. He is the author of numerous articles and stories, and two other books: *Hong Konged* (Adams Media, 2012), a travel memoir, and *General Education Essentials* (Wiley, 2012), a faculty introduction to current trends in liberal education.